R PRESIDENT,

M LINCOLN.

R VICE PRESIDENT,

V JOHNSON.

ND THE CONSTITUTION.

THE
PROCLAMATION
OF
EMANCIPATION,
BY THE
PRESIDENT
OF THE
UNITED STATES,
TO TAKE EFFECT
JANUARY 1st, 1863.

By the President of the United States of America:

A Proclamation.

Whereas, on the twenty-second day of September, in the year of our Lord one thousand eight hundred and sixty-two, a proclamation was issued by the President of the United States, containing, among other things, the following, to wit:

"That on the first day of January, in the year of our Lord one thousand eight hundred and sixty-three, all persons held as slaves within any State or designated part of a State, the people whereof shall then be in rebellion against the United States, shall be then, thenceforward, and forever free; and the Executive Government of the United States, including the military and naval authority thereof, will recognize and maintain the freedom of such persons, and will do no act or acts to repress such persons, or any of them, in any efforts they may make for their actual freedom.

"That the Executive will, on the first day

LINCOLN

THE MAN WHO SAVED AMERICA

LINCOLN

THE MAN WHO SAVED AMERICA

DAVID J. KENT

FALL RIVER PRESS

New York

FOR RU

FALL RIVER PRESS

New York

An Imprint of Sterling Publishing Co., Inc.
1166 Avenue of the Americas
New York, NY 10036

ISBN 978-1-4351-6534-2

Distributed in Canada by Sterling Publishing Co., Inc.
c/o Canadian Manda Group, 664 Annette Street
Toronto, Ontario, Canada M6S 2C8
Distributed in the United Kingdom by GMC Distribution Services
Castle Place, 166 High Street, Lewes, East Sussex, England BN7 1XU
Distributed in Australia by NewSouth Books
45 Beach Street, Coogee, NSW 2034, Australia

For information about custom editions, special sales, and premium and corporate purchases,
please contact Sterling Special Sales at 800-805-5489 or specialsales@sterlingpublishing.com.

Manufactured in China

2 4 6 8 10 9 7 5 3

sterlingpublishing.com

Design by Scott Russo

CONTENTS

Prologue..XIII

Chapter 1: Kentucky Born, Indiana Raised 1

Chapter 2: Coming of Age in Illinois 25

Chapter 3: Beginning a Life in Politics 49

Chapter 4: Lincoln's Loves and Family 73

Chapter 5: Life as a Lawyer 89

Chapter 6: A House Divided—Slavery on the Rise 111

Chapter 7: Running for President 133

Chapter 8: Preserving the Union............................153

Chapter 9: From Gettysburg to Re-election 183

Chapter 10: Of Martyrdom and Legacy 215

Timeline 240

Further Reading and Resources.............................242

Endnotes 250

About the Author 256

Image Credits...256

PROLOGUE

On March 4, 1861, Abraham Lincoln stood beneath the unfinished dome of the United States Capitol, gazing over the gathered crowd with melancholy and trepidation. Erection of the new cast-iron dome, begun six years earlier to replace the old copper-clad wooden one, augured the duties ahead of him: rebuilding the nation. Lincoln was apprehensive, unsure he could accomplish all that awaited him.

The wooden platform constructed on the east side of the building for his inauguration was wet from the morning's rain, and some well-wishers had umbrellas as protection from the continuing drizzle. The gloomy mood was appropriate, as seven states in the Deep South had seceded from the Union in the months since the November election. They would be joined by four more within a few months.

After Lincoln delivered his inaugural address, he was given the presidential oath of office by Chief Justice Roger Taney, whose Dred Scott decision a few years earlier had further divided the nation and enlarged the growing rift between free states and slave states. Lincoln pondered whether he would be able to keep the Union together.

We must not be enemies. We must be friends.

Lincoln tried to reassure the South:

The government will not assail you. You can have no conflict, without yourself being the aggressors.

He pleaded with them not to destroy the vision of the Founders, who established the Constitution "to form a more perfect union." But he was also firm:

You have no oath registered in Heaven to destroy the government, while
I shall have the most solemn one to 'preserve, protect and defend' it.[1]

After being sworn into office, Lincoln traveled alone by carriage up muddy Pennsylvania Avenue to the White House. Just over a month later, the Confederate army fired on Fort Sumter in Charleston, South Carolina, beginning the Civil War. The conflict that followed over the next four years would be the bloodiest and most divisive struggle ever faced by America. The responsibility for saving the nation fell squarely on Lincoln.

OPPOSITE: Lincoln's inauguration at the U.S. Capitol, March 4, 1861; the dome was completed in 1865

Painted from Life
by Thomas Hicks   Springfield Illinois.
June 14th. 1860.

CHAPTER 1

KENTUCKY BORN, INDIANA RAISED

braham Lincoln, namesake grandfather of the future president, was killed by an Indian in the spring of 1786. Thomas Lincoln, the president's father, was nearly killed at the same time. Only 8 years old, young Thomas was being dragged away by his father's murderer when Mordecai, his 15-year-old brother, killed the attacker with a shot from the family musket. Thus Thomas was saved and the family line leading to Abraham Lincoln's birth remained intact. Had Thomas died as a child, the future of the United States would have been substantially different—if the country existed at all.[1]

Thomas was the youngest of three sons, who along with two sisters were left in their bereaved mother's care after his father's death. Through the ancestral law of primogeniture, the entire estate passed to the eldest brother, Mordecai, when he gained adulthood. At that point Mordecai may have turned 12-year-old Thomas out of the house, apparently because of the younger brother's laziness. Thomas

worked as a hired hand to his prosperous Uncle Isaac for a while, until Isaac too disapproved of Thomas's apparent "indolence and improvidence." Left essentially on his own, Thomas became an itinerant laborer, picking up odd jobs wherever he could. These included building roads by hand; clearing brush; plowing, sowing, and harvesting corn; trapping

LEFT: Mordecai Lincoln.   ABOVE: Thomas Lincoln, c. 1800.
OPPOSITE: First painted portrait of Lincoln, by Thomas Hicks (1860)

bear and other food animals; and learning how to build log cabins. Thomas became a reasonably talented (but never profitable) carpenter and cabinet-maker, a handy skill during the winter when planting and harvesting crops was not possible.

Thomas was not particularly well educated. Lincoln would later recall that his father "grew up litterally without education" and could never do "more in the way of writing than to bunglingly sign his own name."[2] Thomas's neighbors saw him as a lazy farmer, preferring to spend his days "hunting, fishing, and loafing rather than farming."[3] When clearing and farming his land, he tended to plant only a small portion of the acreage, just enough to keep his family fed and clothed. This lack of ambition proved to be a major difference between father and son.

In 1806, 28-year-old Thomas married Nancy Hanks, who was six years his junior. Nancy's background is somewhat unclear. It seems likely she was the product of an illegitimate union between her mother, Lucy Hanks, and an aristocratic Virginian planter.[4] When Nancy was around 12 years old, her mother's sister, Elizabeth, married her mother's husband's brother, Thomas Sparrow. After Nancy moved in with the Sparrow family she was known as Nancy Sparrow. In the Sparrow household Nancy learned the basics of housewifery, which included cooking, sewing, and child-rearing, as well as raising crops. Eventually she worked as a seamstress for the nearby Richard Berry family.

ABOVE: The killing of Lincoln's grandfather Abraham, 1786

Thomas Lincoln had been a close friend of Richard Berry, Jr., and so Thomas and Nancy were wed on June 12 in the Berry cabin. Once married, they moved to nearby Elizabethtown in Hardin County, Kentucky, to set up house on the Mill Creek Farm.

Descriptions of Nancy Hanks Lincoln range from tall and pretty to short and homely. Some remembered her as being quiet and subservient to her husband, while others recalled "a bold—reckless—daredevil kind of woman, stepping on to the very verge of propriety."[5] She may have even been a fair wrestler.[6] No known photographs of her exist, and the one painting of her done in 1963 by Lincoln aficionado Lloyd Ostendorf is a stylized portrait perhaps done more from his imagination than any reliable account. Lincoln's law partner and biographer, William Herndon, described Nancy Hanks Lincoln based on an interview after Lincoln's death with cousin Dennis Hanks:

ABOVE: Berry cabin in Kentucky, where Thomas and Nancy Lincoln were married
TOP: Thomas Lincoln loved to sit around and tell stories.

Nancy Hanks Lincoln   Feb. 12, 1963

Lloyd
Ostendorf

She was above the ordinary height in stature, weighing about 130 pounds, was slenderly built, and had much the appearance of one inclined to consumption. Her skin was dark; hair dark brown; eyes gray and small; forehead prominent; face sharp and angular, with a marked expression for melancholy which fixed itself in the memory of all who ever saw or knew her. Though her life was clouded with the spirit of sadness, she was in disposition amiable and generally cheerful.[7]

The couple's first child, Sarah, was born at the Mill Creek Farm on February 10, 1807, a mere eight months after their wedding. Nancy gave birth to Abraham Lincoln a couple years later, on February 12, 1809. In 1812, on yet another farm near Knob Creek, another son, Thomas, was born but lived only three days.

Life on the Farm

Frontier farming was not an easy life. With each move from farm to farm, Thomas had to clear trees to set up a household and plant crops. This was hard labor, and there were few neighbors or friends to help fell hundreds of trees. Trees of requisite sizes—perhaps eight to ten inches across—had to be shaved with primitive hand tools. Logs had to be debarked and, if possible, set out to dry for two years before being used for cabin construction. Logs could be kept round or flattened on the sides. Thomas most likely saddle-notched the ends of the logs so they would fit tightly at the corners. Mud mixed with straw was used for chinking the spaces between logs to keep out rain and cold air. Usually the floor was simply packed dirt. While the cabin had only one room, sometimes it included a sleeping loft reached by wooden pegs inserted in the cabin walls.

Once cleared of trees, the acreage was planted with crops to feed the family. Digging out stumps and roots was a major chore, after which the fields had to be plowed, often by dragging a wooden plow blade behind horses or oxen. Most frontier settlers like Thomas preferred to move during the winter so they could cut logs, clear land, and build rudimentary cabins in time to plant crops in the spring and summer.

Some historians have argued that Thomas was shiftless because he changed farms several times in Kentucky (and, indeed, throughout his life). This is likely

TOP: Dennis Hanks.   ABOVE: William Herndon.   OPPOSITE: Nancy Hanks Lincoln.

an unfair characterization, and several reasons surely exist for Thomas's moves, most notably poor land quality and land-title issues.

When Nancy was heavily pregnant with Lincoln, Thomas moved to Sinking Spring Farm, a 300-acre tract near Hodgenville, Kentucky, named after a spring bubbling up from a sunken cave. He quickly erected a one-room log cabin, barely in time for Lincoln's birth on February 12, 1809. The Lincoln family likely believed this would be an ideal location to raise their growing family, as it had plenty of acreage and was only a few miles from Nancy's aunt and uncle, Elizabeth and Thomas Sparrow.

Within two years, however, the Lincolns were on the move again. While initially idyllic, Sinking Spring turned out to be poor farmland and subject to a legal dispute over the title. After losing his land and his investment, Thomas sought to start over by purchasing 230 acres of land about ten miles away at Knob Creek Farm. Here, Thomas was his most prosperous as a Kentucky farmer. The family again moved into a one-room cabin; planted food crops, including corn and pumpkins; and generally found the farm sufficient to support themselves. When not working the farm or clearing land, Thomas worked as a road surveyor and cabinetmaker.[8]

Sinking Spring Farm, where Lincoln was born and spent his youth

Things were going so well that both Sarah and Lincoln were allowed, at least briefly, to attend local schools.[9] When not in school or laboring on the farm, Lincoln was a typical boy who got into scrapes; corporal punishment from both father and mother was not uncommon. On one occasion he fell into Knob Creek and his playmate Austin Gollaher saved him from drowning. Rather than run home to be coddled in response to the trauma of his near-death escape, Lincoln dried his clothes in the sun for fear his mother would give him "a good thrashing."[10] Later he was kicked in the head by a horse and "apparently killed for a time."[11]

And then yet another land title dispute arose. Even though Thomas purchased Knob Creek Farm and held what he thought was a legal title, outside claimants argued that the land title belonged to them.[12] By 1816 he lost his land again.

Fed up with the lax land-title provisions in Kentucky and unhappy with the presence of slavery in the state, Thomas sold all his remaining land and began planning to move the family again. He made a reconnaissance trip to pick out suitable land, then set out around December 11, 1816, the same day Indiana was admitted into the Union as a free state.

ABOVE: The home where Abraham Lincoln was born, Hogdenville, Kentucky

Indiana

Abraham Lincoln was 7 years old when the family moved to Indiana, and his sister, Sarah, was 9. The Lincolns trekked the 100 miles from Kentucky and settled in the Little Pigeon Creek Community. Thomas felt more confident about his prospects in Indiana. The Land Ordinance of 1785 assured that land titles were secure, a happy change from the chaotic system that governed titles in Kentucky. Indiana was also included in the Northwest Ordinance of 1787, which—among other benefits—banned slavery in what were then known as the northwestern territories (roughly the area now covering Indiana, Illinois, Ohio, Michigan, Wisconsin, and part of Minnesota).

The family settled into the 160 acres of unbroken forest Thomas had staked out earlier in the year. Already a strapping young boy at the age of 7, taller and stronger than average, Lincoln "had an axe put into his hands at once; and from that till within his twenty-third year, he was almost constantly handling that most useful instrument."[13] Indeed, Lincoln joined his father in the male-dominated duties of a new claim, while Sarah learned from their mother about running a household.

The Little Pigeon Creek land offered all the trees needed to construct another one-room log cabin. Even at such a young age, Lincoln became adept at felling trees, shaving them to the proper dimensions, and helping his father build. There was good soil for growing crops and sufficient water access for drinking and farming, as well as accessibility to markets down the nearby Ohio River to sell excess crops. From age 7 to 21 he was occupied helping the family raise hogs, corn, and a variety of other food crops. Thomas also owned horses, which were essential for plowing and harvesting crops, and he settled into a life of farming, carpentry, and hunting.

ABOVE: The Lincoln family moving from Kentucky to Indiana, 1816
OPPOSITE: Lincoln as a young man splitting rails

He acquired additional farmland, became a respected member of the growing community, and was active in the local Baptist church, which he helped build.[14]

Tragedy Strikes

About a year after arriving in Indiana, the Lincolns were joined by Elizabeth and Thomas Sparrow, Nancy's aunt and uncle, and her cousin Dennis Hanks. The three lived briefly with the Lincolns while everyone pitched in to build the Sparrows a cabin of their own. Other families moved into the area, and the community continued to grow.

Everything changed in the early fall of 1818. Both the Sparrows became sick after drinking milk from cows that had eaten the white snakeroot plant, *Ageratina altissima*. There was no known cure for the disease, as the connection to snakeroot and its toxin, tremetol, would not be discovered for decades. Nancy cared for the Sparrows and another neighbor, but there was little she could do, and the Sparrows died. Within two weeks, Nancy came down with the same illness, and on October 5, 1818, she too passed away.[15]

ABOVE: The funeral of Lincoln's mother, Nancy

Lincoln was devastated. Later he reportedly told his law partner and biographer, William Herndon, "All that I am, or hope to be, I owe to my angel mother."[16] At 9 years old, he and his sister were suddenly without their biggest nurturer. Lincoln helped his emotionally distant father build a coffin, and they buried his mother next to the Sparrows in the growing gravesite on the property. Months later, a preacher came through the area and performed last rites at the unmarked grave.

Grieving Lincoln worked even harder in the field to help his father take in the remaining crops for the year and prepare for the long, harsh winter. At only 11 years old, Sarah was forced to take on the duties of a farm wife: cooking the meals, mending the clothes, spinning wool, and maintaining the cabin.

Sarah Bush Johnston Lincoln

As hard as Sarah tried, she was not able to replace her mother. Thomas decided in 1819 to return to Kentucky and find a new wife. Lincoln and Sarah were left behind in Indiana for at least three months, an abandonment that pressed the limits of their young survival skills. In Elizabethtown, where he and Nancy first lived, Thomas found Sarah Bush Johnston, a widow with three children whom Thomas had known many years before. He quickly courted Sarah, whom everyone called Sally, and after Thomas agreed to pay off her minimal debts she accepted his offer of matrimony. They were married on December 2, 1819, and set out on the return trip to Indiana.

By this time, Lincoln and his sister had given up their father for dead, thinking perhaps "some wild animal" had eaten him.[17] When Sally Lincoln arrived, she found the children ragged, dirty, and infested with lice. After rebuking Thomas for leaving them in such a condition, she quickly set to work making the cabin a home. Over Thomas's initial protests, she had insisted on transporting several pieces of furniture from Kentucky to Indiana. The heavy load included a bureau, a table and chairs, a large chest of drawers, cooking utensils, plates and cutlery, a spinning wheel, and two beds, all of which she carefully arranged in the now-

ABOVE: Lincoln helping with the crops

crowded cabin. The family's old furniture, which comprised a few crude stools and smoothed logs, was relegated to the fireplace.

Sally did not stop there: she also insisted that wooden planks be laid over the dirt floor and actual doors and windows be installed. The cabin was scrubbed from top to bottom, as were the children. All this was in an effort to make the cabin a home for the swollen family, which now consisted of Thomas and herself, Lincoln, Sarah, and Dennis Hanks, as well as Sally Lincoln's three children, John, Elizabeth, and Matilda. Another cousin, Sophie, also lived with the family on occasion.[18]

There is no question Sally Lincoln was good for the family. She was an adept seamstress and quickly had Lincoln and Sarah dressed nicely in warm clothes. She was also a skilled cook who served cornbread, wheat bread, and milk from the family cow, and she stewed, fried, or boiled whatever meat Thomas shot on his daily hunting trips, from squirrels to quails and wild turkeys. Occasionally they slaughtered a hog or a hen, the latter of which also gave them eggs. Sometimes she made gingerbread as a special treat for the family.[19]

The large extended Lincoln family settled into their cramped cabin, where they lived for the next eleven years.

Education

In a short biography Lincoln wrote when he was running for president, he admitted his formal education was lacking. He went to school "by littles"—that is, for a few weeks or even days at a time, whenever a teacher might be available.[20]

Lincoln's first education came from his mother, whom he later described as "an intellectual woman, a heroic woman" and "a woman of genius."[21] She introduced him to the Bible, the one book that all households were sure to have. Lincoln studied it intently, memorizing passages he would quote throughout his life.

While still living on the Knob Creek Farm in Kentucky, Thomas sent Lincoln and Sarah to a subscription school. The children walked two miles to a so-called blab school where lessons were read out loud in a single room by all grade levels. Lincoln's first teacher was Zachariah Riney, followed by Caleb Hazel.[22]

Like all farming families, education was secondary to the daily chores, and during planting, tending, and harvesting seasons (essentially early spring to late fall), children were generally not available for education. Lincoln may have also received some unofficial tutoring from Hazel, who lived next door. The siblings' first school experiences lasted only a few weeks, and after moving to Indiana the

OPPOSITE: Young Lincoln and his stepmother Sarah.   ABOVE: Knob Creek Home.

constraints of carving out a new farm from the wilderness, the lack of teachers, and the sickness and death of their mother meant no additional formal education for several years.

Thomas Lincoln had essentially no education, and he was focused on Lincoln helping with the chores. According to Sally Lincoln, Thomas was not against Lincoln learning, but he thought it should never take precedent over farm work. But Sally's arrival marked a change in attitude. She urged young Lincoln to learn. Sally was likely not literate herself, but she encouraged Lincoln to read and write. He became so adept at both that as a teenager he served as an amanuensis for the neighbors.

Lincoln felt he received a fair education in the few weeks he attended school in Kentucky. He perhaps learned a bit more from his second teacher, Caleb Hazel, although Hazel apparently had no qualifications beyond basic reading and writing, augmented by being large enough to successfully thrash any student who got out of line. (This level of teacher training was typical for frontier schools.)

ABOVE: Lincoln at school.   OPPOSITE: *Boyhood of Lincoln* by Eastman Johnson (1868).

Lincoln later noted:

> . . . no qualifications was ever required of a teacher, beyond 'readin, writin, and cipherin,' to the Rule of Three. If a straggler supposed to understand latin, happened to so-journ in the neighborhood, he was looked upon as a wizzard.[23]

In Indiana he again occasionally attended a series of short-term A.B.C. schools. Later he estimated the "aggregate of all his schooling did not amount to one year."[24]

Lincoln made up for this lack of formal education by being autodidactic, teaching himself what he needed to know through extensive reading and talking with any stranger who wandered into town. Aside from the family Bible, he read *Aesop's Fables*, John Bunyan's *Pilgrim's Progress*, Mason Locke Weems's *Life of George Washington*, Daniel Defoe's *Robinson Crusoe*, and *The Arabian Nights*.[25] He borrowed from Josiah Crawford another book about George Washington. After it got wet in a rainstorm, Lincoln worked three days straight for Crawford to pay for the damage. Crawford later gave him the book.[26]

As Lincoln grew older he read Nicholas Pike's *The Complete New System of Arithmetick* and Nathan Daboll's *Schoolmaster's Assistant*. He also used Samuel Kirkham's *English Grammar* and Thomas Dilworth's *A New Guide to the English Tongue*. Later in life his favorite authors were Shakespeare (especially *Macbeth*),[27] Francis Bacon, Robert Burns, and, for fun, the letters of political humorist character "Petroleum V. Nasby" (a pseudonym for journalist David Ross Locke).[28] During his one term as a U.S. congressman, Lincoln "studied and nearly mastered the six-books of Euclid."[29]

Tragedy and Moving On

The Lincoln family had settled into a life in Indiana filled with the usual trials and tribulations of maintaining a cabin, producing enough food to eat and to barter for goods and services, and dealing with the inevitable difficulties of frontier life. At age 19, Sarah fell in love with neighbor Aaron Grigsby, and they were married on August 2, 1826. Eighteen months later, tragedy struck when Sarah and her baby died during childbirth.

ABOVE: Josiah Crawford
OPPOSITE: With no pencils or paper, Lincoln would practice math on a shovel, writing with bits of coal.

LINCOLN AT THE SLAVE
"Boys, let's get away from this," exclaimed Lincoln.

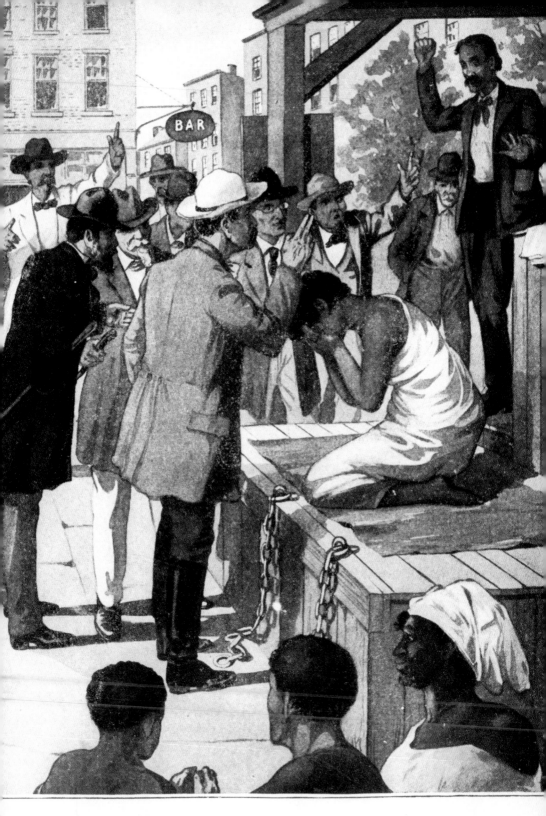

ET IN NEW ORLEANS

er I get a chance to hit that thing, I'll hit it hard!"

Once again, Lincoln was devastated. He blamed the Grigsby family for not calling in a doctor sooner, the doctor for being drunk when he arrived late, and his own father for all the years Lincoln felt he had been treated like a slave. He would not be consoled.

In an effort to escape the pain, Lincoln accepted neighbor James Gentry's offer to join his son Allen on a flatboat trip down the Ohio River, then on to the Mississippi River all the way to New Orleans. The men spent weeks constructing the boat, then loaded it with corn, pork, potatoes, hay, apples, and other commodities. In December 1828 they began their journey. They traveled 1,200 miles over seven weeks, stopping to barter along the way, trading for cotton, tobacco, and sugar they could sell at their final destination.

This trip introduced Lincoln to the issue he would spend much of his life debating. Near a plantation just below Baton Rouge, Gentry and Lincoln were attacked by seven slaves who assumed the two were easy marks for robbery. Gentry and Lincoln put up a valiant struggle, and they managed to scare off the slaves when Gentry pretended to be armed, loudly exclaiming, "Lincoln, get the guns and shoot." In New Orleans, Gentry and Lincoln witnessed a slave auction for the first time. Lincoln told his companion, "Allen, that's a disgrace." This experience set the stage for one of Lincoln's greatest achievements.[30]

After returning to Indiana by steamboat and foot, Lincoln rejoined his family and looked for ways to move on with his life. He was not yet 21 years old and thus remained indentured to his father, who continued to hire him out to neighbors and pocket the proceeds.

Then Thomas decided it was time for yet another move.

PREVIOUS: Lincoln at the slave market in New Orleans
OPPOSITE: A Mississippi River flat-boat and crew on their way to New Orleans

AGAIN THE TEACHERS WERE ALWAYS MEN ---
DERERS WHO USUALLY CAME TO SPEND THE WO
TER MONTHS TEACHING THE LITTLE THEY KNE
XCHANGE FOR FOOD AND OTHER "TRADE".

RITING AND FIGURING IN SCHOOL WAS NOT ENO
O SATISFY YOUNG ABE! HE GOT HIS COUSIN DE

NOTHING WAS TAUGHT BEYOND THE "THREE R'
READING, 'RITING AND 'RITHMETIC; BUT HERE
ABE LEARNED TO DO ALL THREE, IN LESS THA
YEAR'S SCHOOLING UNDER THREE TEACHER

READING BOOKS WAS HIS FIRST INTERES
THEN ON! OFTEN WHEN HE WENT OUT TO WO
FIELD HE WOULD TAKE ONE ALONG TO READ
COLD CORN "DODGERS".

CHAPTER 2

COMING OF AGE
IN ILLINOIS

Abraham Lincoln turned 21 on February 12, 1830. For several years he had anxiously awaited this date, when he no longer had to turn over all his labored earnings to his father. He had first worked as a hired hand outside the family when he was only 13 years old, cutting wood on the banks of the Ohio River with Dennis Hanks and others. He enjoyed this time away, and as he grew older he sought work further from home, usually boarding with the people for whom he toiled. When he was 18, he and John Johnston went to Kentucky and worked on the Louisville and Portland Canal.

Lincoln worked hard when he had to, but despised the drudgery of subsistence farm life, even comparing himself to a slave. He took every opportunity to avoid farm work, seeking the quiet and shade of trees to read any books he was able to obtain.[1] He later admitted "his father taught him to work but never learned him to love it."[2] Lincoln was eager to start life on his own.

Thomas, however, had other plans. He had never understood Lincoln's obsessive reading and learning; he expected his son to remain on the family farm and eventually take it over. But the routine of Indiana was fading into the promise of Illinois, a free state that was rumored to have more fertile land. Dennis Hanks had not fared as well as Thomas in Indiana. His cousin John Hanks had settled in Macon County, Illinois, and convinced Dennis to relocate. Dennis urged Thomas to follow suit, and after a new outbreak of milk sickness in Indiana, Thomas moved on short notice. Less than one month after his twenty-first birthday, Lincoln found himself committed to yet another move to yet another farm in yet another state.

By now the family had reached epic proportions. Thomas, Sally, Lincoln, and John Johnston (Sally's son) joined a caravan consisting of Dennis Hanks; his wife, Elizabeth (Sally's daughter); their four children; Hanks's half-brother, Squire Hall;

OPPOSITE: One of Lincoln's favorite perches was on top of a rail fence.

his wife, Matilda (another of Sally's daughters); and their son. Thirteen extended family members made the journey.

In March 1830 the troop traveled over two hundred miles in homemade wooden wagons pulled by ox teams. They crossed the Wabash River into Illinois, and settled near John Hanks in a wide expanse of timberland and prairie about ten miles west of Decatur. Lincoln and the other men helped Thomas build a log cabin, mauled rails to fence about ten acres of land, broke ground, and sowed a crop of corn.

The first year was brutal. In the fall nearly everyone in the family had become severely ill from mosquito bites and also suffered from ague and fever. Luckily, no one died. The winter of 1830–31 was called the "Winter of Deep Snow." At least three feet of snow fell on Central Illinois, followed by freezing rain and even more snow, which essentially sealed off the family from their neighbors. Lincoln was tasked with tramping through the snow and ice to get corn to the mill, and to claim any unfortunate deer trapped in the ice.[3]

Out on His Own

By the time spring arrived, Thomas was discouraged and reconsidering the move. He packed up the family and headed back toward Indiana, but stopped before he reached the border. He settled in Coles County, Illinois, where he remained for the rest of his life.

ABOVE: The Lincoln family moves yet again

Now 22 years old, Lincoln finally broke with his family. He was hired by Denton Offutt, along with John Johnston and John Hanks, to take a flatboat from Beardstown to New Orleans. Offutt could be described as an entrepreneur-ne'er-do-well who was big on starting things but less enthusiastic about finishing them. On March 1, 1831, Lincoln and the others set off to meet Offutt as agreed in Springfield. On the way they found the melting snows had so flooded the county that walking the saturated, forested land was extremely difficult. Instead, they purchased a large canoe and boated down the Sangamon River.

Offutt agreed to pay each of them $12 per month for the three-month trip; however, he had misrepresented the state of the expedition. Rather than finding a flatboat ready to go, the men encountered Offutt unprepared and holding down a local tavern. The men had to build the flatboat themselves from scratch. Based on his previous experience, Lincoln became the *de facto* captain, even though he was the youngest of the three. He took charge of cutting the timber and constructing the boat. They filled it with the usual cargo, including corn, potatoes, whiskey, and live hogs, the latter of proved more of a challenge than anticipated. Offutt had purchased about thirty "large fat live hogs" and, on a whim, decided that they would be easier to handle if their eyes were sewn shut. After completing the less-than-seamless surgery, they discovered that the now-blind hogs could not

ABOVE: The Lincoln family house in Illinois. FOLLOWING: Lincoln (standing in water with drill) takes charge of rescuing the flatboat that caught on the mill dam.

be driven from the lot onto the flatboat. Eventually, Lincoln tied their legs and hauled them on carts to the boat.[4]

One incident on this trip changed Lincoln's life. As the fully laden flatboat floated down the Sangamon River on the way to meet the mighty Mississippi, the boat hung up on the mill dam outside the tiny village of New Salem. The bow teetered in the air over the dam while the stern dipped low, water seeping into its lower flanks. No amount of effort was able to free it. After assessing the situation, Lincoln took charge of the rescue operation, firing out orders to bring a second vessel nearby. Then he borrowed an auger and drilled a hole in the bow while curious onlookers watched from shore. As he and his crew transferred the cargo to the second vessel, the bow of their flatboat slowly dipped forward, just enough for the water to drain out of the newly made hole, which Lincoln quickly plugged up. The now-lightened load allowed the crew to coax the flatboat over the dam. Soon they were free, reloaded, and back on their way to New Orleans. The townspeople of New Salem were captivated by this spectacle and charmed by the ingenuity of the ungainly stranger they would soon come to know so well.

New Salem

Offutt was so impressed with Lincoln's resourcefulness and take-charge attitude that on the return trip he immediately hired Lincoln to clerk a store he planned to open in New Salem. The village was thriving, with about twenty-five families (roughly 100 people) living mostly in one-room log cabins similar to those in which Lincoln grew up. Offutt's store was one of three in the village, which also included a grocery (aka a saloon), a blacksmith, a cooper (barrel maker), two doctor's offices, a carpenter, a schoolhouse-church, a hat maker, a tanner, an inn, a wool-carding mill, a sawmill and a gristmill, and several residences. This was a centrally located commercial village, and farmers came from miles around to get supplies and trade goods.

In typical erratic form, it took some time before Offutt showed up with stock for the store, so Lincoln hired himself out for any work he could obtain. He again cut rails and helped with farm labor, but also got hired as a river boatman and pilot on the nearby Sangamon River. He served as an assistant clerk on Election Day because he was one of the few people in town who could write. Although new to

OPPOSITE: Lincoln transporting passengers on the Sangamon River

the village, it did not take long for the amiable Lincoln to befriend nearly all its inhabitants. One was the local teacher, Mentor Graham, who hired him as election clerk. Over time, Graham tutored Lincoln in English grammar and took credit for much of his ongoing self-education. As was characteristic for single men, Lincoln never owned a house in New Salem, but instead boarded with Graham and others in exchange for manual labor.[5]

By the end of the summer Offutt finally returned with supplies, and in September he and Lincoln opened the store, selling basic commodities such as coffee, tea, and butter, as well as gunpowder, alcohol, and tobacco. Offutt paid Lincoln $25 a month and allowed him to sleep on a cot in the back of the store with two other assistant clerks. One of the assistants later recalled that he and Lincoln usually slept on the same cot in the cramped space and "when one turned over the other had to do likewise." The men took their meals at the home of Bowling Green, the popular magistrate who lived almost a mile out of town. Green was a farmer and a Justice of the Peace, and he later encouraged Lincoln to study law.[6]

Aside from managing the store, Lincoln and the two assistants were also tasked with running the saw mill and flour mill that Offutt had rented. In addition, Lincoln had to split hundreds of fence rails for a pen to house 1,000 hogs the ever-expansive Offutt had obtained.

Lincoln was a popular store clerk. His long, gangly, and awkward look attracted a lot of attention. He quickly gained a reputation as an honest man who "gave good weight"; that is, he did not shortchange the customers. Graham recalled that Lincoln was attentive to his business, kind and considerate to his customers and friends, and always honest in his dealings. His sense of humor attracted a crowd, as his constant storytelling and joking—skills he learned from his father—kept the citizens lingering.[7]

Perhaps they laughed too much and purchased too little, because in less than a year all of Offutt's businesses in New Salem failed, and he returned to Kentucky to help his more successful brother raise horses. Lincoln was out of a job.

ABOVE: Mentor Graham. OPPOSITE: "What are you studying Abe?" "Law." "Good God Almighty!"

The Black Hawk War

In the spring of 1832, just as Offutt was skipping town, the Black Hawk War broke out in Illinois. Black Hawk was a chief of the Sauks, a Native American tribe that had crossed the Mississippi River into Illinois from the Iowa Indian Territory. Black Hawk was planning to resettle land that the U.S. government had taken as part of an 1804 treaty. Black Hawk felt the treaty was unjust. With him were about 450 warriors and 1,500 women and children. The government called on Illinois to form a militia to repel what they considered a hostile act.

Lincoln volunteered with sixty-seven other men from the New Salem area to join the battle. Once he arrived at the muster site, Lincoln's friends pushed him to run for the position of captain. Soldiers voted by forming a line behind one of two candidates, Lincoln or the prosperous sawmill owner William Kilpatrick. To Lincoln's great surprise, more men lined up behind him, and he became Captain of the Volunteers. In his presidential campaign autobiography, he characterized this event as "a success which gave me more pleasure than any I have had since."[8]

OPPOSITE: Lincoln managing the store
ABOVE: Lincoln hears the call for four hundred volunteers to fight in the war.
FOLLOWING: People of New Salem offer cheers and farewells as Lincoln and his men leave for the campaign

Lincoln saw no action during the brief war, which was fortunate given how little he knew about military strategy or terminology. At one point he needed to get his men through a gate in a fence but "could not for the life of me remember the proper word of command for getting my company endwise so that it could get through the gate, so as we came near the gate I shouted 'The company is dismissed for two minutes, when it will fall in again on the other side of the gate.'"[9]

After one month of largely uneventful service, the 1,400-member volunteer army disbanded. Given that he had no job to return to, Lincoln re-enlisted along with about 300 others, this time as a private. A young Lieutenant Robert Anderson mustered Lincoln back into service. Three decades later Anderson was in command of Fort Sumter, whose shelling by the Confederate army started the Civil War. In June, Lincoln re-enlisted again, this time as a private in Dr. Jacob Early's Independent Spy Company. These few months were the extent of Lincoln's military experience, and while he saw no action, he did witness some of the brutality of war during

OPPOSITE: Black Hawk, leader and warrior of the Sauk American Indian tribe
ABOVE: Lincoln's company discovers a dozen scalped militiamen.

several incidents in which his company came across dead and scalped soldiers. After his service, Lincoln headed back to New Salem to find gainful employment.

Back to Work

When he returned from the Black Hawk War, Lincoln had no means of employment or income. He briefly considered learning blacksmithing, but he also wanted to further his education, which he acknowledged was sorely lacking. Around this time New Salem resident James Herndon sold his interest in the general store he owned with his brother Rowan to William F. Berry, who had served with Lincoln in the militia. Dissatisfied with Berry, a few weeks later Rowan sold his own share to Lincoln. Berry was the son of a Presbyterian minister from an influential family, so may have paid for his share, but Lincoln's share was obtained on credit. In 1832, Berry and 22-year-old Lincoln were suddenly partners, store owners, and in debt.[10]

The store came fully stocked with the usual items, just as Offutt's outfit had been. Mostly they served farmers coming in from the surrounding territory. When another store failed, Berry and Lincoln quickly scooped up the extra goods. The new products included a barrel of whiskey, which teetotaler Lincoln avoided but Berry proved all too fond of. This may help explain the store's lack of profits.

Business was slow, and Lincoln was generally left to operate the store while Berry worked his second job as town constable or was away attending college. The slow pace was perfect for Lincoln, who much preferred entertaining to selling, often sitting by the fire telling humorous stories and jokes to anyone who might wander inside. Everything from the weather to politics was ripe for intense discussion, and Lincoln kept all his visitors enthralled. He freely extended credit to his growing list of friends, which seemed to include everyone who walked into the store.

In early 1833 Berry and Lincoln bought a larger store across the road. Here the two men, likely at Berry's urging, applied for a license to sell whiskey by the glass. Lincoln would have to walk a fine line of denial in his debates two decades later with Stephen A. Douglas, who negatively referred to Lincoln being a "grocery-keeper," or bar-owner.

New Salem had begun to stagnate as a community, in large part because the nearby Sangamon River was not as navigable as hoped. The combination of too much competition, the overstocking of supplies, and inexperienced management by both owners put the business in a bad financial position. In 1834, the store "winked out."[11] Not long afterward, Berry grew severely ill, most likely from a life of hard drinking, and died. Lincoln was forced to assume the considerable remaining debts of the failed business, which totaled more than $1,000 ($27,000 in today's valuation). He jokingly referred to this as his "national debt," and it took him many years to repay.

OPPOSITE: The country store in New Salem.   TOP: Lincoln studying law while "keeping store."

Other Jobs

Even when the store was bringing in business it was insufficient to cover the meager costs of Lincoln's day-to-day life. During his nearly six years in New Salem, when not sleeping at the store he boarded with a series of locals.[12]

Lincoln took on other jobs to cover his minimal bills. He paid $1 to $2 per week for room and board, and perhaps up to $1.50 a month for basic seamstress and laundry services. Often he worked in trade rather than pay directly.

The ease with which Lincoln made friends came in handy. In the spring of 1833 he secured an appointment as postmaster of New Salem, a patronage job assigned by President Andrew Jackson. Although Jackson was a Democrat and Lincoln had started to think of himself as a Whig, Lincoln later acknowledged that the job was "too insignificant, to make his politics an objection."[13] Mail arrived only twice per week, so the job did not pay well, but Lincoln held the position until the post office closed three years later. He was one of the few people who could handle the paperwork, which included quarterly reports to Washington.

More important than the pay was access to the news. In addition to the occasional letter, Lincoln received all the newspapers from the East, including the major papers from Washington, D.C., New York, Philadelphia, and Boston. His habit was to carefully peruse each paper before delivering them to their subscribers. This allowed him to learn about important local and national issues.

Later in 1833, complementing his postmaster work, Lincoln was also hired as assistant surveyor to John Calhoun, surveyor of Sangamon County. Lincoln had no experience in the field, so he borrowed two surveying books from Calhoun: Abel Flint's *A System of Geometry and Trigonometry: Together With a Treatise on Surveying* and Robert Gibson's *A Treatise on Practical Surveying.*[14]

ABOVE: Lincoln as a surveyor. OPPOSITE: Lincoln making his rounds as postmaster.

Lincoln was determined to teach himself surveying. He purchased the required equipment—a compass and chain, marking pins, stakes, plumb bobs, and an axe—and set off to survey much of the northern part of the country under the direction of Calhoun and Thomas Neale, Calhoun's primary assistant. Lincoln's financial well-being improved, although much of his surveying equipment was obtained on credit and he still owed a substantial part of his own "national debt" from the winked-out store.

ABOVE: Lincoln splitting rails during the time he was studying to become a surveyor
OPPOSITE: Lincoln's interest in politics steadily grew.

THE GROWING LEADER

For two years Lincoln surveyed everything from home sites to roads, racetracks, and entire towns in the wide sprawl of Sangamon County. He quickly gained a reputation as both an excellent surveyor and a trustworthy man who could be counted on to be accurate and fair with all parties.

During much of this time in New Salem, Lincoln was also pursuing another goal that would prove to be much more lucrative and important to humanity: politics.

...AN IN THE REGION COULD SWING AN AXE SO HAR...
...AKE A BIGGER CHIP FLY THAN YOUNG LINCOLN...
...D.   AND LIKE MOST YOUTHS, ABE WAS NOT...
...HFUL ABOUT SHOWING OFF.

...METIMES A GATHERING OF LOCAL YOUTHS R...
...FREE-FOR-ALL FIGHT.   IF INJUSTICE...

AT EVERY HOUSE RAISING HIS GREAT STRENG
IN DEMAND, AND AT THE FEASTING AND PLAY W
USUALLY FOLLOWED SUCH AN AFFAIR, LINCO
GREATLY ENJOYED HIMSELF.

T· THERE WAS PRANKISH FUN IN HIM, TOO. O
PICKED MUDDY-FOOTED URCHINS OUT OF A
AND LET THEM "WALK" ON THE CEILING OF

CHAPTER 3

BEGINNING A LIFE IN POLITICS

During Lincoln's first year in New Salem he joined the rather pretentiously named Literary and Debating Society, which was actually an informal discussion group run by James Rutledge. A well-respected leader in town, Rutledge was father of ten children and proprietor of an inn, Rutledge's Tavern. He also had a personal library of nearly thirty books (quite an extensive collection for the time and place), which became one of Lincoln's favorite hangouts.

By this time Lincoln was well known as someone always ready with a funny story or ribald joke. But in his first debating effort he surprised the audience with a thoughtful, well-reasoned, analytical presentation. Rutledge was impressed, later telling his wife that "there was more in Abe's head than wit and fun, that he was already a fine speaker; and that all he lacked was culture to enable him to reach the high destiny which he knew was in store for him."[1]

Reaction from townspeople was so positive that in March 1832 Lincoln put his name into contention for the Illinois state legislature. He composed a lengthy announcement titled "Communication to the People of Sangamo County," which was published in the *Sangamo Journal*.[2] In it, he laid out his political philosophy, which was astonishingly well-rounded for a 23-year-old man raised on frontier farms. That philosophy largely mimed the American System originated under Alexander Hamilton and promoted by Henry Clay, whom Lincoln later eulogized as his "beau ideal of a statesman."[3]

The American System was an economic philosophy premised on three mutually reinforcing pillars: a high protective tariff, a national bank, and federal subsidies for internal improvements (roads, canals, railroads). The goal was to facilitate the development of transportation infrastructure and strong markets, particularly

OPPOSITE: Lincoln proved a surprisingly adept politician.

for rural farmers who were cut off from much of the market economy. While a stable two-party system had not yet fully developed, the American System quickly became the mainstay of the Whig party in opposition to the policies of Democratic President Andrew Jackson. Lincoln later asserted he "had always been a Whig" (that is, until he was a Republican).

In response to local concerns, Lincoln noted he was not (yet) in favor of railroads because their costs outweighed the benefits. But referring to his own experience on flatboats, he strongly supported improvements to the navigability of the Sangamon River, which was so important to New Salem. Presaging his future as an analytical thinker, Lincoln went into great depth in his discussion of why river navigation presented a more efficient economic opportunity than railroads. He also spoke up against usury, the loaning of money at exorbitant interest rates, and emphasized the importance of central banking.

Finally, while not dictating any specific system, he stressed that education was "the most important subject which we as a people can be engaged in," stating that his wish was that "every man may receive at least, a moderate education."

This was an extraordinary treatise for a man who had only recently moved into the county. Lincoln mentioned that his "peculiar ambition" was to be "truly esteemed of my fellow men, by rendering myself worthy of their esteem," but also seemed to understand that he had a slim chance of winning a seat, noting "if elected [the independent voters of this county] will have conferred a favor upon me," but that if he lost he had "been too familiar with disappointments to be very much chagrined."[4]

He lost.

It is not clear whether Lincoln was chagrined over this defeat. Immediately after publishing his announcement to enter the race, he volunteered for service in the Black Hawk War. This left him only a few weeks upon his return to canvass the outer portions of the county, while his many competitors had the entire summer. However, even with those deficiencies he won 277 of the 300 votes cast in New Salem. This was testament to Lincoln's popularity, especially considering that support came from a precinct that overwhelming voted for Jackson's reelection that year (Lincoln was a well-known backer of Jackson's opponent,

TOP: Andrew Jackson.　ABOVE: Henry Clay.

Henry Clay). In his 1860 Presidential campaign biography, Lincoln took solace in the fact that this was the only time he was ever "beaten on a direct vote of the people."[5] It would not, however, be the last time he lost an election.

Illinois State Legislature

When the election of 1834 came around, Lincoln again ran for the state legislature. This time he took advantage of the wanderings facilitated by his postmaster and surveying duties to meet as many voters in the county as possible. His Black Hawk War service had also given him many important and useful contacts.

Once again, Lincoln supported the Whig position of internal improvements, a strong central bank, protective tariffs, and readily available public education. He favored construction of a canal between Beardstown and the Sangamon River, which would improve health conditions by eliminating stagnant pools and create a way for New Salem–area farmers to transport produce to the Illinois River, their primary route to eastern and southern markets.[6] Mostly, however, Lincoln focused on making himself better known in the county.

Lincoln helping in the fields

On one occasion, in Island Grove, Lincoln came upon a group of men harvesting crops. They told him he would gain their support if he helped with their work. "Well, boys," Lincoln said, "if that is all then I am assured of your votes…" He then picked up some tools, and jumped in to help for several hours. He got their votes.

Lincoln was in his element as a rural campaigner, touring on horseback the farms spread around the county, telling humorous stories and chatting about the farmer's hopes and dreams, crops and planting practices, and the schools their children attended. Because of his own experience on farms he could ingratiate himself with all manner of potential voters, from rich to poor. He also had an affinity for children, often picking them up and telling jokes to keep them happy while he conversed with everyone in the family.

All of this retail campaigning worked in Lincoln's favor; he won 1,375 votes, the second-highest total of any of the candidates. Fellow canvasser and Black Hawk War veteran John T. Stuart also won a seat. Lincoln was reelected in 1836, 1838, and 1840, serving eight years in the legislature over four terms. He later noted that "members of the legislature got four dollars a day, and four dollars a day was more than I had ever earned in my life."[7] He was about to become one of the leading Whigs in the state of Illinois.

Internal Improvements

Before Lincoln could attend to his first day as a new legislator, he had to buy some decent clothes. Always awkwardly dressed, he frequently wore pants that ended six inches before his shoes started. He asked to borrow some money from a friend, Coleman Smoot, who lent Lincoln $200, some of which he used to purchase his first professionally made suit. Lincoln duly repaid the loan as soon as he was able.[8] Now appropriately outfitted, Lincoln joined three dozen other first-time legislators in the state capital of Vandalia.

Lincoln kept his day job as surveyor because the Illinois legislature was essentially part-time employment: the first session ran from December 1, 1834, to February 13, 1835. As a member of the minority anti-Jackson faction—which in 1838 would officially become the Whig Party—Lincoln was largely an observer during his first term. When he won reelection in 1836, he was joined by eight other legislators from Sangamon County (two senators and seven representatives), all of

OPPOSITE: Lincoln talking politics with a farmer.

whom were at least six feet tall. The group came to be known as the "Long Nine," both for their heights and their level of influence. Given that about three-quarters of his fellow lawmakers were unsophisticated farmers (the remainder were lawyers), Lincoln stood out as having an analytical mind and being relatively well read. His status quickly grew, and he became the leader of the Long Nine and began managing the legislative program of the Whig minority.[9]

Although he was the youngest of the Long Nine, Lincoln garnered the most votes in the election, and with one term as representative completed he was accepted

as their leader. The Long Nine included notables like Ninian W. Edwards (son of a former Illinois Governor), Daniel Stone (who signed with Lincoln on the slavery protest discussed in the next section), and John Dawson (a veteran lawmaker and hero of the Indian wars).[10]

While generally keeping his head down as a freshman legislator (voting with his mentor John Stuart virtually every time), Lincoln was not completely inactive. Within two weeks of beginning the first session, he introduced a bill authorizing the construction of a toll bridge over Salt Creek in Sangamon County. The bill passed. Recognizing his strong writing skills, other legislators called on Lincoln to help draft their bills.

It is not surprising that Lincoln's first bill was related to building infrastructure: he was acting on behalf of voters back in his district and jumping into the internal improvement debate that was dominating the session. Among other bills designed to set up a system of internal improvements—the building of roads,

Mr Speaker
    I now give notice that Thursday
next. or some day thereafter I shall ask leave
to introduce a bill entitled an act to au=
thorize Samuel Musick to build a toll bridge
across Salt Creek in Sangamon county—

TOP: Ninian Edwards. ABOVE: Lincoln's bill authorizing construction of the Salt Creek toll bridge.

canals, railroads, and navigable rivers—was one to construct the Illinois and Michigan Canal. The canal would run from Chicago, then only a small port of about 2,000 people on Lake Michigan, to LaSalle, thus providing a connection via the Illinois River through to the Mississippi River and New Orleans.[11]

Lincoln strongly supported all internal improvements, most emphatically the Illinois and Michigan Canal, for which he would serve as a commissioner many years after his state legislative terms were over. He approved hiring William Gooding, engineer on the Erie Canal in New York, as chief engineer on the canal. Lincoln told his friend and confidant Joshua Speed that "his highest ambition was to become the DeWitt Clinton of Illinois."[12] DeWitt Clinton had been Governor of New York State in the early 1800s and was directly responsible for the construction of the Erie Canal. While there had been initial concerns about the

costs of construction, Clinton's canal project was a huge success, carrying vast amounts of passenger and freight traffic and providing an economic boom for the state. Lincoln hoped for the same in Illinois.

The reality of the Illinois canal plan was more problematic. In December 1835, Governor Joseph Duncan, a former Democrat who had only recently switched to the Whig Party, called for a special session of the Illinois state legislature to deal with the growing management and funding problems of the internal improvement program. In an effort to build support and satisfy impatient voters in their home districts, the legislature had spread the placement of projects widely throughout the state. This led to the development of roads, railroads, canals, and navigation projects that were random rather than systematic. For example, rail lines would be installed for a few miles near one developer's interests but then stop, so the railroad effectively went nowhere. During the special session, Lincoln was able to fund his own pet project, a corporation to build a canal between Beardstown and the Sangamon River. He even bought land near its terminus in anticipation of increased development. Unfortunately, the canal was never built.[13]

TOP: Joshua Speed. ABOVE: DeWitt Clinton. FOLLOWING: Satirical illustration of the Panic of 1837.

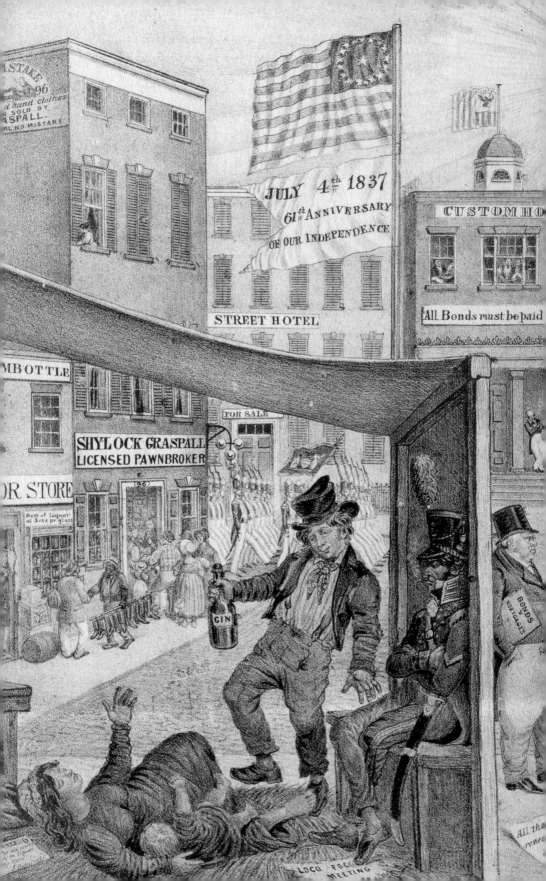

Funding for the internal improvement system continued to be problematic, largely because of financial speculation in the East that caused economic instability throughout the country for years. Both the Democratic (including Stephen A. Douglas) and Whig parties had initially supported the Illinois internal improvement program, but after the Panic of 1837 effectively dried up cash flow and put the state in serious debt, the Democrats withdrew their support. That left Lincoln and his fellow Whigs virtually alone in trying to keep the programs going.

As the primary leader of the Whig agenda, Lincoln proposed several options to fund the internal improvement scheme statewide, but eventually he had to narrow the focus to funding the Illinois and Michigan Canal. The Canal finally opened in 1848, but the state continued to pay the backlogged debt for many decades.

From Vandalia to Springfield

While debate raged over canal and railroad construction, another issue consumed much of Lincoln's time: the location of the capital. Vandalia had been the state's capital since 1819, prior to which the capital had been the flood-prone Mississippi River–banked city of Kaskaskia. Illinois had been populated largely from south to north, with much of the population migrating from Kentucky (just as Lincoln's family had done). But by the 1830s the state's population had shifted even further north as a result of continued immigration from southern states and movement from New York and New England. (This westward move was partly facilitated by the Erie Canal completed under DeWitt Clinton. Today, Illinois features DeWitt and Clinton Counties, and the county seat of DeWitt is the city of Clinton.)

Vandalia was quickly proving inadequate as a capital city for reasons other than its less-than-central location. Its population was less than 900, so when legislators were in town they strained the capacity of lodgings and eateries, not to mention the city's ability to rid the muddy streets of horse manure. Many of the men newly elected to the legislature found the city dull and dreary, lacking—among other pleasures—enough women to enlighten the evening social scene. Transportation to the city from across the state was poor and often impassable for several months a year. Sickness was ubiquitous during the summer; five legislators died there between 1830 and 1836.[14]

ABOVE: Governor Orville H. Browning

To the farm-raised Lincoln, Vandalia offered some intellectual stimulation, including bookshops. There were also lectures given at the antiquarian and historical society and by professors from McKendree College, including one from an officer in Napoleon's army. Other intellectual leaders sponsored parties, dances, and receptions in an attempt to enliven society. Lincoln spent many social evenings with state senator Orville H. Browning and his wife, and Browning became an important ally throughout the remainder of Lincoln's life.

As much as Vandalia tried to be a good host, the capitol building was already falling apart. Although only a decade old, the capitol was "manifestly inconvenient for the transaction of public business." Plaster was falling from the ceiling, bricks were crumbling, floors were sagging, walls were bulging—all the result of hurried construction on inadequate ground. A desperate attempt to keep the legislature in Vandalia led to building of a much sturdier—and uglier—new capitol building in 1836.[15]

By this time, however, there was a concerted push to relocate the capital to a more central location. The original move to Vandalia came with a stipulation that another move would be forbidden for twenty years, or until 1839. Several other cities contended for relocation, including Alton, Decatur, Peoria, Jacksonville, and Springfield. Lincoln led the fight for Springfield, located in his home district in Sangamon County.

TOP: John C. Calhoun. ABOVE: Erie Canal.

Springfield had originally been named Calhoun after South Carolina Senator John C. Calhoun. The senator fell out of favor after he became a southern pro-slavery firebrand, however, so city leaders changed its name in 1832 to Springfield (after the city in central Massachusetts). About seventy-five miles north of Vandalia, the city already had a population of several thousand and was on a plateau of firm, flat ground well suited for construction.

After the relocation bill was introduced in the state house, there was considerable wheeling and dealing in an effort to get support for Springfield. Lincoln and the Long Nine were accused of "logrolling," the practice of vote trading. The other dominant issue at the time was internal improvements, so the Lincoln-led group promised to support various improvement projects throughout the state in exchange for legislators' support for moving the capital to Springfield. It was generally accepted, at least in private quarters, that the exchange of money might help convince some lawmakers to vote a particular way. But the ever-honest Lincoln apparently did not employ this strategy. According to his closest friend, Joshua Speed, when Lincoln was given $200 to grease the palms of hesitant lawmakers, Lincoln returned all but seventy-five cents of it, explaining "I didn't Know how to Spend it."[16]

Springfield was not as hard a sell as anticipated, and required little special effort in politicking. Many hailed Springfield as a perfect site because of its central location in an ever-growing state population (Chicago was a small town with little sign of its future greatness). Orville Browning, who while doggedly opposing the internal improvement plans, nevertheless drafted the relocation bill and guided it through the state senate. On February 28, 1837, a joint session of the General Assembly agreed to designate Springfield as the new state capital, effective in 1839.[17] Lincoln, who continued to live in New Salem through his first three terms as a state legislator, relocated to Springfield for his final term.

Introduction to Slavery

One other issue played a relatively small role in Lincoln's time in the state legislature. Although the Illinois constitution banned slavery, it did have highly restrictive "black laws" that effectively limited the ability of free blacks to live and work in the state. At the same time, abolitionists who wanted a nationwide ban

OPPOSITE: Illinois House journal entry on anti-aboliton resolution and slavery, by Lincoln and Dan Stone

the words "and other purposes".—

Ordered that the title of the bill be as amended, that the Clerk inform the Senate thereof, and ask their concurrence to the amendment of the House to said bill and the title thereof.

The following protest was presented to the House which was read and ordered to be spread on the Journals,—namely.—

Resolutions upon the Subject of Domestic Slavery having passed both branches of the General Assembly at its present Session, The undersigned hereby protest against the passage of the same.

They believe that the Institution of Slavery is founded both in Injustice and bad policy; but that the promulgation of Abolition Doctrines tends rather to Increase than to abate its evils,

They believe the Congress of the United States has no power, under the Constitution to Interfere with the institution of Slavery in the different States,

They believe that the Congress of the United States has the power, under the Constitution to abolish Slavery in the district of Columbia; but that that power ought not to be exercised unless at the request of the people of said district,

The difference between these opinions, and those contained in the said Resolutions, is their reason for entering this protest".—

      Dan Stone,
      A. Lincoln,

Representatives from the County of Sangamon.

A Message from the Council of Revision by Mr Ewing the Secretary.
    Mr Speaker,
      The bills entitled,
"An act to Incorporate the Colhoun Coal and Mining Company"
"An act for the Formation of Michigan County"
"An act laying out certain State Roads"
"An act to Incorporate the Chippawa Dry dock Company"
"An act to Incorporate the Peoria Hotel Company,"
Have been approved of by the Council of Revision.

on slavery were gaining strength and influence. This led pro-slavery forces to push for anti-abolition resolutions. While Lincoln abhorred slavery—he later said, "I am naturally anti-slavery. If slavery is not wrong, nothing is wrong"—he also felt the abolitionists were doing more harm than good.[18]

When the Illinois legislature passed an anti-abolitionist resolution in 1837, Lincoln was one of only six house members to vote against it. To clarify this seemingly counterintuitive position, he later wrote a protest, co-signed by Dan Stone, one of the Long Nine who was not seeking reelection. In the protest, the two men made clear they believed:

> . . . that the institution of slavery is founded on both injustice and bad policy; but that the promulgation of abolition doctrines tends rather to increase than to abate its evils.

And further, he said they believed:

> . . . that the Congress of the United States has no power, under the constitution, to interfere with the institution of slavery in the different States.[19]

Lincoln wanted everyone to understand he was anti-slavery, but also felt bound by the Constitutional restrictions on taking action against the "peculiar institution." These were fairly radical thoughts for a young western legislator, and would set the stage for Lincoln to become a national leader on the issue of slavery.

Lincoln Goes to the U.S. Congress

After serving his fourth term in the state legislature, Lincoln was looking for more challenging opportunities and did not run for reelection. In 1838 he campaigned for John T. Stuart, who beat another young Illinois politico, Stephen A. Douglas,

TOP LEFT: Stephen A. Douglas. TOP RIGHT: John J. Hardin. ABOVE LEFT: Edward D. Baker. ABOVE RIGHT: John T. Stuart. OPPOSITE: Abolitionist broadside quoting Thomas Jefferson.

ONE HOUR OF
American Slavery

Is Fraught With More

MISERY

Than Ages of that which we rose in

REBELLION
TO OPPOSE.

THOMAS JEFFERSON

for a seat in the United States Congress. In early 1843 Lincoln decided to run for the newly created Seventh Congressional District.

But he had rivals: fellow Whigs and close friends John J. Hardin and Edward D. Baker, the latter for whom he named his second son. Lincoln withdrew from the race because he thought Baker had an insurmountable lead, but in the end the

seat went to Hardin. A sort of gentlemen's agreement was resolved in which the three party elites would serve single terms in rotation. Hardin won his race and served his term, followed by Baker. Despite Hardin's attempt to renege on the arrangement, Lincoln was the Whig candidate in 1846 and, as agreed, served one term as a U.S. congressman from December 1847 to March 1849.[20]

This was Lincoln's first time in Washington, D.C., or in any large city other than his brief flatboat visits to New Orleans. At the time, Washington was a mix of formal government buildings and run-down boarding houses, and was a constant quagmire of mud and filth. The roughly 40,000 inhabitants were squeezed into a District area newly shrunken by the return of the Alexandria portion south of the Potomac River to the Commonwealth of Virginia. Slavery pens sat within eyesight of the Capitol building, which was still capped by a rotting wood and copper dome. Lincoln and his family lived at Mrs. Sprigg's boarding house on 1st Street SE in a spot now covered by the Jefferson Building of the Library of Congress.

Joining him were eight other members of Congress, all with abolitionist tendencies, so Lincoln likely had many interesting debates about slavery over the common dinner table.

Most of his congressional duties were mundane, such as answering letters from constituents and voting on appropriations, but Lincoln's good humor and adeptness with a funny story ingratiated him with his fellow representatives. Not long after his arrival he wrote back to his law partner, William Herndon, that he was "anxious" to "distinguish" himself in this august body.

Not content with merely making speeches on immaterial subjects, instead he chose to take on the President of the United States.

TOP: William Herndon. MIDDLE: James K. Polk. ABOVE: Zachary Taylor.

President James K. Polk had initiated a war with Mexico that would eventually result in the United States gaining territory encompassing present-day Texas, New Mexico, Arizona, Colorado, Utah, Nevada, and California. George Ashmun, a Whig member of the U.S. House of Representatives, offered an amendment to what had been expected as a perfunctory commendation to those who served in the war. The amendment proposed to add a coda to the resolution: "In a war unnecessarily and unconstitutionally begun by the President of the United States." Lincoln voted in favor of the amendment, which passed 82 to 81.[21]

Lincoln went a step further. Polk insisted Mexico had been the aggressor, but Whigs believed that was an invention to hide Polk's desire to expand the United States (and, by extension, the area to which slavery could be instituted). Three days before Christmas, Lincoln introduced a series of eight interrogatories demanding President Polk identify the exact spot where Mexico had supposedly initiated the first bloodshed. Because Lincoln repeatedly asked the spot be identified, they became derisively known as the "spot resolutions."

ABOVE: Lincoln's "Spot Resolutions"
FOLLOWING: 1847 map of Mexico including California & the Southwest. Texas gained statehood in Dec. 1845.

MAP OF MEXICO,

INCLUDING

YUCATAN & UPPER CALIFORNIA,

exhibiting

THE CHIEF CITIES AND TOWNS, THE

Principal Travelling Routes &c.

PHILADELPHIA:

Published by S. Augustus Mitchell

N.E. CORNER OF MARKET AND SEVENTH Sts

1847.

Entered according to the Act of Congress in the year 1846 by S. Augustus Mitchell, in the Clerks office of the District Court of the Eastern District of Pennsylvania

Scale of Miles

THE LATE BATTLEFIELD.

A. American Battery
B. Cathedral
C. Bishop's Palace
D. Heights above it
E. Fort opposite side of the River
G. 1st Fort
H. 2d Fort
K. 3d Fort, covering the Causeway Road
L. Main Plaza
M. Cemetery

MONTEREY

Corn Fields

Cultivated

Cultivated Land

TEXAS

GULF
OF
MEXICO

BAY OF CAMPECHE

YUCATAN

CARIBBEAN
SEA

CUBA

GUATIMALA

GULF OF HONDURAS

CITY OF MEXICO

Not surprisingly, Polk completely ignored the impertinent demands of an unknown freshman representative from the western prairies. Lincoln pressed the point, and Polk continued to ignore him, as did virtually everyone in Congress. The spot resolutions faded away without any debate or action, but Lincoln had asserted himself as unafraid to challenge even the highest authorities. He showed the integrity and determination to change the status quo and make things right. Later the spot resolutions would come back to haunt him when Democrats ridiculed him as "spotty Lincoln," which may have hurt his chances to get a land office patronage job.[22]

Lincoln immersed himself in other issues during his one term in Congress, including his proposal for emancipation of the slaves in the District of Columbia (although it was never formally introduced or passed). After his first session he toured New England campaigning for Zachary Taylor as the Whig nominee for president, even though Taylor had been a hero of the Mexican War. He then took a roundabout route past Niagara Falls through the Great Lakes by steamship, and along the newly opened Illinois and Michigan Canal on his way back to Springfield.[23] He was essentially removed from politics for several years while he focused on his family and his law practice.

OPPOSITE: N. C. Wyeth's 1919 painting of Lincoln delivering his second inaugural address

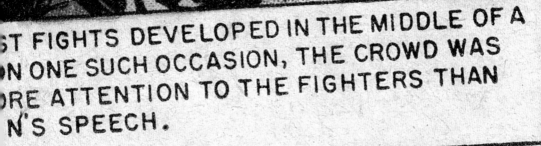

ST FIGHTS DEVELOPED IN THE MIDDLE OF A
N ONE SUCH OCCASION, THE CROWD WAS
RE ATTENTION TO THE FIGHTERS THAN
N'S SPEECH.

OWERFUL HANDS HOISTED THE MAN INTO
AND TOSSED HIM ASIDE --- ENDING THE
L, AND WINNING FOR ABE THE ADMIRATION

TO CONVINCE THE FARM VOTERS THAT HE
ONE OF THEIR OWN KIND, ABE MIXED FIEL
WITH SPEECHES.   ONE OF HIS HUGE F
COULD BURY A MAN ON THE LOAD!

CHAPTER 4

LINCOLN'S LOVES AND FAMILY

Abraham Lincoln was not a ladies' man. The consensus about him when he was a teenager in Indiana was that "he was not much attracted to girls." His reticence did not change after he arrived in New Salem. He remained, as fellow New Salemite Jason Duncan noted, "very reserved toward the opposite sex." Another friend noted that Lincoln rarely "went out with the girls" and "was not very fond of girls." Lincoln's cousin John Hanks said, "I never could get him in company with women; he was not a timid man in this particular, but he did not seek such company." Colleague Judge David Davis provided an outlier opinion, suggesting to William Herndon that Lincoln indeed had a strong passion, but that his conscience kept him from seducing women. Overall, however, it seemed Lincoln was not particularly interested in pursuing romance.[1]

The reasons for Lincoln's disinterest stem from three main factors: his physical awkwardness, his lack of classical education, and his inclination to be the center of attention in social situations. At six-feet-four-inches tall and thin as a rail, Lincoln towered over most of his friends and was physically ungainly. His voice tended toward a high-pitch squeakiness that belied his size. He could neither sing nor dance. His face was often described as homely, at best, and his normal attire reflected both his lack of financial standing and attention to detail. Because he was self-taught—still incomplete at this stage of his life—he could not maintain the kind of intellectual discussion with women he desired, and he found less intellectual women too frivolous. As a storyteller and rail-splitter, he enjoyed entertaining with jokes and feats of strength. These pursuits were solely the realm of men, and Lincoln felt more comfortable in the company of men.[2]

OPPOSITE: Mary Todd Lincoln. ABOVE: Judge David Davis.

Lincoln did have his share of romantic entanglements, however. Some women claimed he had shown interest in courting, but they rejected him as unsuitable for marriage. One pitied his awkwardness and apparent ineptitude with women. Another thought him too gangly and did not like his "Indiana accent." A third also found him "not much of a beau," and suggested he "seemed to prefer the company of the elderly ladies to the young ones."[3]

Lincoln and the Married Ladies

Indeed Lincoln did seem to prefer spending time with older married women, sometimes to the dismay of their husbands. He boarded with Bowling Green while building the flatboat for Denton Offutt, and near the Green house was that of Bennett Abell and his wife, Elizabeth. Lincoln got along well with both Abells—he voted for Bennett and another friend, Jack Armstrong, for two constable positions—but he latched on to Elizabeth Abell as a sort of surrogate mother. In the fall of 1833, when Lincoln was surveying the Petersburg area, he boarded with the couple. A friend of Lincoln's credited Mrs. Abell with giving Lincoln the idea he might improve himself by reading and studying.

He looked up to other mature married women as well, including Mary Spears, Mrs. John Camron, and Hannah Armstrong. Hannah was the wife of Jack Armstrong, the leader of the Clary Boys, a rough, hard-drinking gang who wandered New Salem making trouble just to alleviate the boredom. Jack had challenged Lincoln to a wrest-ling match soon after his arrival. Differing accounts of the match call it either a Lincoln win or a draw, but when it was over Jack and the gang all respected him. Later, Lincoln had a close relationship with Eliza Browning, wife of legal and political colleague Orville H. Browning. Yet another surrogate mother figure was Sarah Graham, wife of Mentor Graham, who played a significant role improving Lincoln's English grammar. According to Sarah's daughter Elizabeth, Lincoln talked to Sarah about a wide variety of topics, including love and other personal matters.[4]

Ann Rutledge

Part of their conversation on love likely concerned Ann Rutledge, whom Lincoln first met as a fellow student of grammar in the Graham household. Much has been said about the relationship between Ann Rutledge and Abraham Lincoln,

OPPOSITE: Lincoln and Ann Rutledge in Lincoln's store

and yet it remains one of the mysteries of his life. The relationship first came to light only after Lincoln's assassination, when William Herndon began extensively interviewing and writing to everyone who had known Lincoln. Herndon so sensationalized the relationship in an 1866 lecture that it offended Lincoln's remaining family. Later biographers seeking to humanize Mary Lincoln downplayed the much earlier Ann Rutledge romance to the point where even today it is difficult to discern reality from mythology.[5]

This much we know. Ann was the daughter of one of New Salem's founders, James Rutledge, the same man who sold the goods from his own failed store to Berry and Lincoln and who ran the Literary and Debating Society. Four years younger and more than a foot shorter than Lincoln, Ann was a cherubic 130 pounds, considered "a woman of Exquisite beauty," and had a "Mouth well Made beautiful" and "good teeth." More important to Lincoln, she was "studious" and "ambitious to learn," and had an intellect "quick" and "sharp." To him, she possessed "the brightest mind of her family." Always attracted to intelligent and strong women, Lincoln later described Ann to an old friend as "natural and quite intellectual, though not highly educated." He admitted that he loved Ann dearly, noting she would have "made a good loving wife."[6]

However, Ann was already engaged to John McNamar (who also went by an alias, McNeil), a relatively prosperous merchant who co-owned a general store with Sam Hill in New Salem. After a disagreement with Hill, McNamar went back east, ostensibly to fetch his family from New York. He did not return for three years. During that time the Rutledges moved to a farm in Sandridge, a few miles out of New Salem. Lincoln visited often, and a budding romance emerged between the left-behind Ann and Lincoln, although the courtship was hindered by the uncertainty of whether McNamar would ever return. Lincoln helped Ann with her chores, studied Kirkham's *Grammar* with her, and accompanied her on long walks in the evening light. According to Ann's brother Robert, Ann and Lincoln became informally engaged, pending a final determination of McNamar's intentions and the opportunity to inform him of her change in feelings so she could obtain an honorable release.

Apparently Ann considered joining her brother at Illinois College in Jacksonville, but in the summer of 1835 she came down with what her sister called "brain fever" and was probably typhoid. Within weeks, on August 25, 1835, she was dead. Once again, as when his mother and sister had died, Lincoln was devastated. He "became plunged in despair," and his friends feared for his sanity. They kept a close watch on him for weeks, even taking away his pocketknife to ensure his safety. The depths of his grief were beyond imagination. Elizabeth Abell, with whom he was boarding at the time, said she had never seen a man mourn for a companion as much as Lincoln did for Ann Rutledge.[7]

Mary Owens

Another, almost comical, romance involved Mary Owens, the sister of Elizabeth Abell and a cousin of Mentor Graham. Prior to his apparent courtship with Ann Rutledge, Lincoln met Owens when she was in New Salem visiting her sister. After she left, he perhaps jokingly, and certainly at Elizabeth Abell's insistence, agreed to court Mary if she returned to the area. Lincoln thought Mary Owens to be "intelligent and agreeable, and saw no good objection to plodding life through hand in hand with her."[8]

Three years later, about a year after Rutledge's death, Mrs. Abell told Lincoln she was heading home to Kentucky for a visit and would bring back her sister Mary for Lincoln to wed. Oddly enough, the 27-year-old Lincoln agreed to this proposition. Perhaps he did not expect Mary to return on such a whim, but she did, and he was in a bind.

Mary had put on significant weight since they had first met. While Ann Rutledge was cherubic, Mary filled out her proportions—at five-feet-five-inches she now weighed a portly 180 pounds. While perhaps more intellectually sharp and educated than Ann, Mary was dignified but more matronly in appearance. Lincoln immediately had second thoughts about plodding through life with her. Not surprisingly, Mary also had doubts. While Lincoln was now serving in the state legislature, he was still "deficient in those little links which make up the great chain of woman's happiness."[9]

But Lincoln had made a commitment to Mrs. Abell, and he felt obligated to go through with it. Later recalling to Eliza Browning, Lincoln wrote:

> But what could I do? I had told her sister that I would take her for better or for worse; and I made a point of honor and conscience in all things, to stick to my word, especially if others had been induced to act on it, which in this case, I doubted not they had, for I was now fairly convinced, that no other man on earth would have her, and hence the conclusion that they were bent on holding me to my bargain.... At once I determined to consider her my wife; and this done, all my powers of discovery were put to the rack, in search of perfections in her, which might be fairly set-off against her defects.

Following a courtship of letters in which Lincoln seemed to be trying to talk her out of it, he proposed marriage to Mary Owens. She said no. Shocked and more than a little embarrassed, he repeated his proposal several times. Each time she turned him down. By May 1837 they agreed the marriage idea was a bad one and had no further correspondence. Mary eventually married Jesse Vineyard and moved to Missouri; their sons later joined the Confederate Army.

Feeling rather abashed about the whole affair, Lincoln told Eliza Browning in 1838:

> Others have been made fools of by the girls; but this can never be with truth said of me. I most emphatically, in this instance, made a fool of myself. I have now come to the conclusion never again to think of marrying; and for this reason; I can never be satisfied with anyone who would be block-headed enough to have me.[10]

ABOVE: Mary Owens

Joshua Speed

Of course, Lincoln did again think of marrying. In 1837, as he was officially breaking up with Mary Owens, Lincoln moved to Springfield. He had been in the Illinois state legislature for three years and was ready to move up from the village of New Salem, which was already starting to decline. With the negotiations over moving the capital from Vandalia to Springfield under way, the move was advantageous.

But he was broke. Even with his full pay for the last session of the state legislature in hand, Lincoln rode his old horse to Springfield deep in debt. Upon arrival, one of his companions on the trip, William Butler, sold Lincoln's horse without

telling him, paid off his debts, and moved his saddlebags into the Butler household about fourteen miles out of town. Lincoln continued taking his meals at the Butlers without charge for the next five years. After a while Lincoln decided he needed to find a place in town, and he rode in on a borrowed horse with his saddlebags, a few law books, and the clothes on his back seeking residence. His first stop was Joshua Speed's store. According to Speed, Lincoln asked "what the furni-

ture for a single bedstead would cost." Putting slate to pencil, Speed told him the sum would be seventeen dollars. Taken aback, Lincoln agreed it was probably a fair price but replied, "If you will credit me to Christmas, and my experiment here as a lawyer is a success, I will pay you then. If I fail in that I will probably never be able to pay you at all." Seeing his forlorn look, Speed offered:

I think I can suggest a plan by which you will be able to attain your end, without incurring any debt. I have a very large room, and a very large double-bed in it; which you are perfectly welcome to share with me if you choose.

ABOVE: Joshua Speed. OPPOSITE: Mary Todd Lincoln with a lock of her hair.

"Where is your room?" asked Lincoln. Speed pointed to the stairs leading from the store to his room. Saying nothing, Lincoln took his saddlebags, went up the stairs, tossed them on the floor, and returned "beaming with pleasure" to say: *"Well, Speed, I'm moved."*[11]

Lincoln shared the room with Speed for the next three-and-a-half years, often with other store clerks and assistants. One such clerk was a very young William Herndon, who later went into partnership with Lincoln. The atmosphere was jovial, and Lincoln was his usual story-telling self. Speed became Lincoln's closest friend and confidant for the rest of his life, even though Speed eventually returned to his slave-holding family in Kentucky. As was common between men of those days, the two shared their most intimate vulnerabilities, a relationship that rivaled any of Lincoln's romantic loves. When Speed questioned his affection for the woman he was about to marry, Lincoln helped him through the doubts. Later, when Lincoln was going through the same process, he turned to the happily married Speed for advice. He was seeking counsel regarding his relationship with Mary Todd.

Mary Todd

The fourth of seven children, Mary Todd was born in Lexington, Kentucky, to a wealthy slave-holding family. Her mother died when she was only 6 years old. Within two years her father, Robert Smith Todd, remarried and had another nine children with his new wife. Mary Todd and her siblings all had difficult relationships with their stepmother, who essentially ignored them while favoring her own

growing brood. Despite these difficulties, Mary grew up in comfort and privilege. The celebrated statesman Henry Clay owned a plantation called Ashland down the road from the Todd household. When she was 13, Mary rode her new pony to Ashland, and Clay, the perennial presidential candidate, noted to his guests, "If I am ever President I shall expect Mary Todd to be one of my first guests." The precocious Mary said she would enjoy living in the White House.[12]

Robert Todd was rather progressive for a nineteenth-century southern slave owner, and he encouraged his daughters as well as sons to get an education. In part because her stepmother wanted her out of the way, 14-year-old Mary was sent to live at Madame Mantelle's finishing school for young ladies. There she received a classical education that concentrated on French and literature. She became fluent in French and also studied dance, drama, music, and, of course, the social graces needed to attract a suitable husband. Unlike most women of the time, she also took a keen interest in politics, becoming both knowledgeable and ambitious—and Whiggish. But like all women, politically she had to live vicariously through her husband.[13]

In the fall of 1839 Mary moved from Kentucky to Springfield to live with her older sister Elizabeth, who had married Ninian W. Edwards, son of the former governor of Illinois. The Edwards home was the center of Springfield's social scene, and given that the city had far more single men than eligible women, their home was the place to shop for a well-heeled husband. Mary was in her element. Her advanced education gave her the advantage of choosing which of her many suitors she might spend time with, among them Stephen A. Douglas and Abraham Lincoln.

Joshua Speed invited Lincoln to one of the Edwards' soirées. Although Lincoln's six-foot-four-inch lankiness towered over Mary's five-foot-two-inch roundness, the two began courting over the winter of 1839–40. The courtship was somewhat one-sided. Lincoln remained a rough, uncouth, awkward man who alternated between sitting quietly and blurting out inappropriate *faux pas*. He was charmed by Mary's knowledge and wit, often staring at her in apparent awe as she led the conversation. Still, she saw something in him and their unlikely courtship blossomed, with Mary doing most of the courting.

Initially supportive, Mary's family (in particular, her sister Elizabeth) came to oppose the mismatch, feeling Mary could do much better. Lincoln was deeply hurt by this opposition, but the two continued to see each other and eventually became engaged.[14]

OPPOSITE: Slaves in the cotton field

A Hiatus

Then they stopped. Somewhere between late 1840 and early 1841 Mary and Lincoln abruptly, although mutually, called off the engagement. Many agreed that Lincoln backed out, fearing he could not suitably meet any wife's needs as a husband because of his distracted nature. Whatever the reason, they were no longer courting throughout 1841 and into 1842.

A contributing factor may have been that in late fall of 1840 Lincoln had tumbled into love with Matilda Edwards, the younger cousin who was also staying at the Edwards home in Springfield. While Lincoln had been courting Mary (or vice versa), Joshua Speed had been interested in Matilda. The two men joked that Lincoln would marry Mary and Speed would wed Matilda. But Matilda had other ideas and, finding Speed unsuitable, she unceremoniously rejected him. At this point Lincoln may have thought of himself as a potential mate for the more affable and coquettish Matilda, but apparently he never made any particular move; many years later Matilda claimed not to have any knowledge of his affections.[15]

During this hiatus, Lincoln also proposed to Sarah Rickard, whom he had met when they were both living at William Butler's home outside of Springfield. Rickard, like Owens, turned him down, partly because of their age difference (her 16 to his 32) and because of his "peculiar manner and his general deportment."[16] Once again, Lincoln was having no luck with the ladies.

Marriage and Family

Sometime in 1842 Mary and Lincoln began secretly courting again. Despite Elizabeth's opposition, the two often met at the Edwards house and sat on the low couch for hours, talking about life and love. They also probably discussed politics, as by this time Lincoln was actively involved in Whig party activities and Mary was as ambitious as he, perhaps even more so. Their romance bloomed again, enough that Mary flirtatiously and anonymously wrote a letter backing up Lincoln's own anonymous letter to the local paper mocking James Shields, a political rival. Shields, feeling his honor had been attacked, challenged Lincoln to a duel. Lincoln tried to back out of it, but when Shields insisted, the tall and muscular Lincoln offered up heavy broadswords as weapon of choice. Faced with a severe disadvantage, the short-armed Shields allowed himself to be talked out of the fight.

To the astonishment of the Springfield social set, Lincoln and Mary suddenly decided they would get married—that night. Elizabeth Edwards claimed the wedding occurred with only two hours' notice, and indeed the marriage license was issued that very day. Lincoln had a "deer in the highlights" look as he approached the hurried ceremony in the Edwards parlor. According to friends, when Lincoln was dressing for ceremony he was asked where he was going, to which he replied, "I guess I'm going to hell." At least one Lincoln scholar believes Mary may have seduced Lincoln the night before into doing something that obligated him to marriage.

Whatever the reason, the two were married on November 4, 1842. A week later Lincoln seemed resigned to the fact, closing a business letter with, "Nothing new here except my marrying, which to me, is matter of profound wonder."[17]

Regardless of whether Mary seduced him, the pair welcomed their first son, Robert Todd Lincoln, into the world on August 1, 1843. Three more sons followed Robert: Edward Baker on March 10, 1846, William Wallace on December 21, 1850, and Thomas on April 4, 1853. Robert was the only son to reach adulthood.

Edward, whom the Lincolns called Eddy (or Eddie, according to the Park Service at Lincoln's Tomb in Springfield), was named after Lincoln's friend, colleague, and political mentor, Edward D. Baker. Eddy lived only a few years, dying a month before his fourth birthday of consumption, a common cause of death in the nineteenth century. The actual disease may have been tuberculosis or some form of thyroid cancer.

Despondent over the death of their son, Mary became pregnant again within a few weeks. The rambunctious William, aka Willie, helped fill the void left by the death

TOP: Edward Baker Lincoln.   ABOVE: Mary, Willie, and Thomas (Tad) Lincoln.

of the older brother he would never meet. Willie accompanied his parents to Washington when Lincoln became president. The city was a dangerous place during wartime because of the hordes of soldiers and southern sympathizers, not to mention the poor health conditions resulting from the mosquito-infested swamps abutting the Executive Mansion. The heat, humidity, and pestilence drove Lincoln out to the Old Soldier's Home north of town during the summer. But Willie died of typhoid in the White House on February 20, 1862. Both Lincoln and Mary were devastated. While Lincoln threw himself into waging the Civil War, Mary never completely recovered and wore black for the rest of her life.

Robert Todd Lincoln

Thomas was named after Lincoln's somewhat estranged father, but everyone called him Tad because as an infant he had a large head and was as wiggly as a tadpole. Tad was born with a partial cleft palate that was not externally noticeable but gave him a lisp and made his speech difficult to understand. He and Willie ran ramshackle over the White House until Willie's premature demise. Tad enjoyed wearing military uniforms and "playing soldier," much to the chagrin of the White House staff and cabinet. Lincoln was incredibly lenient with his boys, perhaps to relieve his guilt when Willie died or to make up for rarely being home during Robert's childhood. Tad survived his father's assassination and his mother's near-insanity only to die at 18 years old when a common cold developed into severe damage to his lungs.

Robert went on to be the closest guardian of his father's legacy, controlling all his papers and directing the epic biography written by Lincoln's two White House secretaries. He served two presidents as secretary of war and a third as ambassador to the Court of St. James (United Kingdom), as well as Counsel and then President of the Pullman Palace Car Company (train sleeper cars). He married another Mary and witnessed two more presidential assassinations. He died a wealthy and accomplished man in 1926 at the age of 82. Robert is the only family member not buried in the Lincoln Tomb in Springfield, Illinois; at his wife's insistence, he was placed in a large aboveground sarcophagus in Arlington National Cemetery across the river from the Lincoln Memorial.

Many people characterized Abraham and Mary Lincoln's relationship as difficult—she once chased him out of the house with a knife and was insanely jealous of any woman who even spoke to him—but their marriage somehow worked. Their rare letters show a loving couple discussing the usual family issues—financial matters, health, the well-being of their children—and reveal even mild flirtatiousness.[18] Despite the angst of observers, even their most vehement detractors admit that the pair loved each other through all their trials and tribulations.

BLY THEY DID NOT NEED TO SAY MUCH TO
OTHER, BECAUSE THEIR UNDERSTANDING
DEEP. AND PROBABLY THEY BOTH ACCEPTED
ACT THAT THIS WAS GOODBYE.

'S MOURNING WAS A PRIVATE MATTER, BUT
RUTLEDGE, THE YOUNG COUSIN WHO HA

LESS THAN A WEEK LATER THEY LAID ANN R
TO REST IN CONCORD'S FRONTIER CEMETER
AND NOBODY REMEMBERED SEEING ABE LIN[
AMONG THE MOURNERS.

THREE WEEKS AFTER ANN RUTLEDGE'S F
HER VANISHED FIANCÉ, JOHN McNAMAR, R
TO N[ ]W SALEM WITH HIS MOTHER.   HOW

CHAPTER 5

LIFE AS A LAWYER

While still working as a postmaster and surveyor in New Salem, Lincoln started dabbling in the law. During his successful 1834 campaign for the Illinois state legislature, he often went out on the stump with established lawyer John T. Stuart, who also won a seat. Stuart and Lincoln had known each other since the Black Hawk War. Impressed by Lincoln's logic, Stuart encouraged him to study the law and lent him some law books. But Lincoln's interest had actually started much earlier, when he was still in Indiana.

Lincoln earned his first dollar working as a ferryman on the Ohio River. One day he was ferrying two gentlemen from the river's Indiana banks to a steamship waiting in the middle. Once aboard, they each tossed him a silver half-dollar. This gave Lincoln confidence. But then brothers on the Kentucky side of the river sued him for trespassing on their license to ferry patrons across the river. The legally untrained Lincoln pled his own case, arguing that he had not violated their rights because he had ferried customers only halfway across the river. The judge agreed and dropped the charges.

While boarding with Bowling Green in New Salem, Justice of the Peace Green encouraged Lincoln's intellectual curiosity by letting him attend sessions of his court. Green lent Lincoln some law books, which he read during the slow times while clerking in Offutt's store. Given the dearth of lawyers in New Salem, Green let Lincoln practice in his court, relishing the spectacle of a young, frumpily dressed, unlicensed rail-splitter arguing cases. Over time his mirth gave way to appreciation for Lincoln's logic and ability to home in on the key points of the cases.[1]

OPPOSITE: Early daguerreotype of Lincoln the congressman, 1846

Law Partner #1: John T. Stuart

But Lincoln was not licensed to practice, so Green was actually aiding and abetting an illegal act. Encouraged by Green and inspired by Stuart, Lincoln began studying the law in earnest before starting his first session of the state legislature. The first law book he read was William Blackstone's *Commentaries on the Laws of England*, commonly known as Blackstone's *Commentaries*. In the early to mid-nineteenth century there was little in the way of precedent, which governs most modern legal proceedings today. Especially in the West (including Illinois), trials were carried out more as works of art than legally robust jurisprudence. Blackstone's *Commentaries* provided the bridge between the English law on which U.S. laws were largely based and the special circumstances inherent in the U.S. Constitution and common law. To that was added frontier common sense.

Lincoln followed Blackstone by reading Joseph Chitty's *A Practical Treatise on Pleadings*, Joseph Story's *Commentaries on Equity Jurisprudence*, Simon Greenleaf's *A Treatise on the Law of Evidence*, James Kent's *Commentaries on American Law*, and the Revised Statutes of Illinois. When a colleague in Springfield asked the best way to gain knowledge of the law, Lincoln advised him that the long and tedious process was to "get the books and read," insisting to young lawyers that

"work, work, work, is the main thing."[2] And work he did. Soon he was drafting legal documents like deeds for his less literate neighbors in New Salem.[3]

Lincoln's studies were interrupted during sessions of the legislature, but by the fall of 1836 he had obtained his license to practice law. He had to wait until March 1 of the following year to be admitted to the bar. Becoming a lawyer at that time, especially in the rough frontier of Illinois, was not as rigorous as it is today. Like many western lawyers, Lincoln simply read the books—he never attended classes or college like the more

ABOVE: John T. Stuart
OPPOSITE: Justice Bowling Green presides over one of Lincoln's early trials over ownership of a hog.

elitist lawyers in the East did. Passing the bar involved being quizzed on knowledge of the law and demonstrating "good character." Well-respected Springfield lawyer Stephen T. Logan gave Lincoln a certificate vouching for the latter, and his exam was likely a literal walk in the park with the examining official to gauge his worthiness. By April 15, 1837, he had relocated to Springfield, moved in with Joshua Speed, and become Stuart's junior partner.[4]

Stuart left much of the work to Lincoln while he pursued his political ambitions. A state legislator like Lincoln, in 1839 Stuart won a seat in the U.S. House of Representatives and began spending a good deal of time in Washington. When not in state session himself, Lincoln had all the legal work he could handle. Mostly he collected promissory notes, which were still the primary means of purchasing products and services in the days before reliable cash. Of the 4,000 cases in which Lincoln is the attorney of record, more than 2,500 were some form of debt collection. Receipts were small, usually $5 or $10 a case, but the number of cases filed led to a steady income for the junior attorney, especially given that Stuart shared the proceeds equally.[5]

Law Partner #2: Stephen T. Logan

When Stuart was reelected to Congress in 1841, the partnership was dissolved. Lincoln entered a new partnership with Stephan T. Logan, the man who had assured his moral fortitude when he first became a lawyer. Logan had recently disbanded his partnership with Edward D. Baker, the man after whom Lincoln would later name his second son. Looking for someone as eloquent as Baker to complement his own more intellectual reticence, Logan saw a perfect opportunity with Lincoln. Logan was nine years older than Lincoln, and had established himself as a preeminent attorney in Sangamon County after being equally respected in his native Kentucky. He was serving as a judge in the circuit court when he vouched for Lincoln, but grew dissatisfied with the meager pay and returned to private practice. He saw in Lincoln someone who would be "exceedingly useful to me in getting the good will of the juries," the one area where Logan was weaker because of his cracking voice and peevish demeanor.[6]

It was a good match for Lincoln, too. Logan had a sharp analytical mind and a command of legal precedents and technicalities. In contrast, while adept at working a jury, Lincoln was rather lazy in his study of the finer points of the law. Like Lincoln, Logan was not overly concerned about his physical appearance;

he was more likely to be leaning back in his chair, "his hair standing nine ways from Sunday, while his clothing was more like that worn by a woodchopper than anybody else."[7]

Lincoln continued doing mostly debt collection cases, but he now received only one-third of the money paid to the firm, as Logan had a less egalitarian profit-sharing policy. But whereas Stuart was largely absentee, Lincoln learned a great deal about the business of the law from Logan. Most critically, he began to understand the importance of detailed case research

ABOVE: Stephen T. Logan. OPPOSITE: View of the east side of Springfield Square with the county courthouse at left (behind tree with peaked roof), where Lincoln tried dozens of cases
FOLLOWING: Springfield Street, where Lincoln's law office was located

and preparation. Lincoln was inherently logical in thinking, but Logan taught him to write more precise and succinct case readings. Gone was the flowery language so common in that age; instead Lincoln learned to break down the case into its critical components. Under Logan he learned to search out precedents and watch for technical aspects that could be used in his clients' favor. He still avoided thorough reading of law books—William Herndon would later say that he "never knew him to read through and through any law book of any kind"—but he did "love to dig up the question by the roots and hold it up and dry it before the fires of the mind."[8]

The firm of Logan and Lincoln was dissolved in 1844, when Logan decided to go into practice with his son. Now an experienced country lawyer, Lincoln decided it was time he became senior partner.

Law Partner #3:
William H. Herndon

Lincoln had known the Herndon clan all the way back to New Salem. James and Rowan Herndon had sold their shares of a store to William Berry and Abraham Lincoln. (Rowan, who married the sister of Mentor Graham, shot and killed his wife in a mysterious incident that was ruled an accident.) William Henry Herndon, whom Lincoln called Billy, was their cousin. Lincoln had known Billy Herndon from his days living at Joshua Speed's store; Billy also worked there as a store clerk and shared the room upstairs with Speed and Lincoln. He had also "read" the law at the firm of Logan and Lincoln, just as Lincoln had previously read with Stuart.[9] Still, Herndon was taken aback when Lincoln one day walked into his

ABOVE: William H. Herndon
OPPOSITE: Former law office of Lincoln and Herndon, covered in funeral bunting, 1865

office and asked, "Billy, do you want to enter into partnership with me in the law business?" Herndon had yet to get his law license (although he did shortly afterward) and had no real experience, so Lincoln's choice was curious. On the other hand, Lincoln was tired of being the junior partner and wanted someone who would be better at office management, an area where he was wholly deficient. He saw Herndon not so much as an adroit lawyer but "a laborious and studious young man" who would be efficient keeping the books. They also were compatible on politics; Herndon was an ardent Whig, although primarily a behind-the-scenes organizer with little interest in running for office.[10]

Despite occasional battles with the bottle, Herndon was indeed a diligent junior partner. More impulsive and spontaneous in his reactions than the thoughtful Lincoln, Herndon nevertheless became a critical complement and a willing colleague. As junior partner to Logan, Lincoln had received less than

ABOVE: Lincoln the lawyer

half of the money brought into the firm, even when he was the one who did all the work. As the senior partner in his own firm, Lincoln was more democratic, splitting all receipts equally with Herndon—even in cases where Lincoln brought in and completed the work before telling Herndon they had it. In grateful return, Herndon ran the office; built an extensive library of historical, philosophical, and scientific treatises; and oversaw all the students who came in to read the law. He also kept the law business going when Lincoln was out on the circuit. Lincoln did make one misjudgment in his initial hiring of Herndon: he turned out to be a much better lawyer than Lincoln anticipated.

Life on the Circuit

While Lincoln officially practiced law in Springfield, he also spent six months every year riding the circuit. Circuit riding provided legal services to the masses in need. A judge, several lawyers, and occasionally some assistants traveled a circuit route from one county seat to another. At each stop they spent a week or two handling any cases in need of trials. They generally did this for three months in the fall and three months in the spring.[11]

Lincoln and Logan initially rode the First Judicial Circuit, but then Sangamon County was included into the new Eighth Judicial Circuit, which was the mainstay of Lincoln's legal career until he was elected president. The Eighth District covered much of central Illinois, from Shelby, Christian, and Sangamon counties in the south to Livingston County in the north. From west to east it ran from Menard and Mason counties to Vermillion and Edgar counties. The exact county makeup changed over time as population growth (or decline) caused some counties to be added, subtracted, combined, or split, but no matter which counties were included, Lincoln got to know them very well.[12]

The circuit began in Springfield, Lincoln's home and county seat of Sangamon County. It then moved to Tazewell County, followed by Woodford, McLean, and Logan and continuing on throughout the Eighth Circuit until circling back to Springfield. All told, the Eighth Circuit covered more than 11,000 square miles.[13]

Until 1839 the presiding judge on the circuit was Samuel Treat, after which David Davis, the prominent attorney and jurist from Bloomington, took over the judgeship duties. Davis and Lincoln became great friends, with Davis later leading Lincoln's supporters to Chicago for the 1860 convention. Lincoln generally partnered with one of the other lawyers for more complex cases, but most of the time his client's opponent hired them as legal adversary to Lincoln. Over time Lincoln

ROLLIN

became so respected by his fellow lawyers that he sat in as judge, including as many as ninety-five cases in 1858 alone.

Before railroads, the men made the grueling trip on horseback. When reaching a river they were obligated to cross without benefit of bridges or ferries, plunging into the typically cold water in the hopes their horses could find a suitable place on the other bank to rise out. Later, the increasingly hefty Davis rode in a horse-drawn carriage out of sympathy to any horse whose back might have to carry him. The westernmost counties offered long stretches of monotonous prairie grass. Dust and heat during the warmer months were common, as was biting cold and the occasional blizzard in early spring and late fall. Upon arriving in the county seat the lawyers picked up any waiting business, generally with only a perfunctory meeting with their client on the courthouse lawn before walking in to try the case.[14]

While the travel was exhausting and the accommodations were often wretched, Lincoln appeared to thrive during his months riding the circuit. When railroad service had spread enough to make going home on weekends feasible, Lincoln was the only attorney to stay out on the circuit between work sessions. The opportunity to meet the local populace, tell humorous stories, and read whatever books he could find was advantageous to his off-and-on political career, not to mention often preferable to the erratic demands of Mary Lincoln back home.

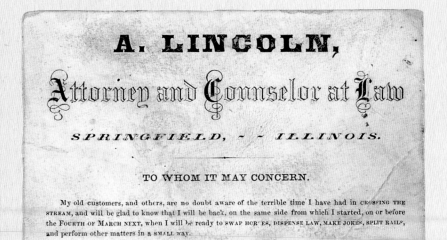

A. LINCOLN,
Attorney and Counselor at Law
SPRINGFIELD, ~ ~ ILLINOIS.

TO WHOM IT MAY CONCERN.

My old customers, and others, are no doubt aware of the terrible time I have had in CROSSING THE STREAM, and will be glad to know that I will be back, on the same side from which I started, on or before the FOURTH OF MARCH NEXT, when I will be ready to SWAP HORSES, DISPENSE LAW, MAKE JOKES, SPLIT RAILS, and perform other matters in a small way.

OPPOSITE: Lincoln riding the circuit.   ABOVE: Lincoln's business card.

Caseload

Aside from the debt collections that made up much of Lincoln's caseload, he also handled many divorces and other relatively simple cases that required little preparation and were decided according to principles of right and wrong. Most of his early practice was community based and involved people he knew. He often served as a mediator or peacemaker in disputes, urging people to forego litigation and settle their differences. Around 1850, he told budding lawyers to always be honest, and if you "cannot be an honest lawyer, resolve to be honest without being a lawyer."[15]

As his career grew he took on more complex cases and those from out-of-state interests. He had fewer community-based cases and more market-oriented litigation. He took on more corporate clients, albeit reluctantly, as he never completely adapted to the faster pace and impersonal style.[16]

But to think in terms of debt and corporate cases is to underestimate the breadth of Lincoln's law business. Over his twenty-five-year career as a litigator his caseload included "a staggering variety of cases involving arbitration, assault and battery, bad debt, bankruptcy, bastardy, bestiality, breach of marriage, divorce, impeachment of an Illinois justice, insanity, land titles, libel, medical malpractice, murder, partnership dissolution, patent infringement, personal injuries, property damages, rape, railroad bonds, sexual slander, slave ownership, and wrongful dismissal."[17]

A handful of important later cases give a sense of the kind of logical thinking that set Lincoln apart from other lawyers and positioned him to play such a critical role in saving America from itself.

Almanac Murder Trial

One such case was a murder trial. In 1857, William "Duff" Armstrong and James Norris were charged with the murder of James Metzker during a drunken brawl outside New Salem. Norris allegedly struck Metzker on the back of the head with a three-foot-long piece of wood. Meanwhile, Armstrong purportedly used a slung-shot (a metal mass attached to a flexible handle or strap) to strike Metzker in the right eye hard enough to cause his death. Norris, unable to afford his own attorney, was immediately tried and quickly convicted of the crime. Armstrong, the son of Abraham Lincoln's old Clary Boys friend Jack Armstrong, was granted a separate trial and a transfer to a less inflamed jurisdiction. When the case was finally tried, Lincoln volunteered to be Armstrong's attorney without pay.

OPPOSITE: Lincoln defending Armstrong at his trial

During cross-examination Lincoln nonchalantly walked the key prosecution witness through his description of the scene. The witness insisted he was able to see clearly the alleged murder from a distance of 150 feet at 11 p.m. The reason for such clarity? The full moon was shining brightly, "as high in the heavens as the sun would be at ten o'clock in the morning." After a brief recess, Lincoln returned to his cross-examination, this time pulling out the *Ayer's American Almanack*. Opening it to the correct date, he had the witness read the pertinent sections, which showed that the moon was not full, but barely past the first quarter. The almanac also stated the moon had disappeared by 11 p.m. As such, it was too dark to see anything from so far away. After the jury was sent back to deliberate, Lincoln told Armstrong's mother, "Aunt Hannah, your son will be free before sundown." He overestimated; the jury found Armstrong not guilty within the hour.[18]

Manny/McCormick Reaper Trial and His Own Patent

This trial is important even though Lincoln never tried the case. Because of his interest in technology, Lincoln was often called in on patent cases. One such case was the McCormick reaper case. As populations grew the need for improved crop yields increased, and the mechanical reaper made that possible. Cyrus McCormick sued John Manny for patent infringement, accusing him of stealing McCormick's reaper design. Manny's lawyers called in Lincoln because of his jury skills and his local presence in Illinois, but then the case was transferred to the district court in Cincinnati, Ohio.

Lincoln spent considerable time preparing for the case and writing a technical brief. But when he arrived in Cincinnati he was shocked to learn that an esteemed Ohio lawyer, Edwin Stanton, had been hired and Lincoln's services were no longer

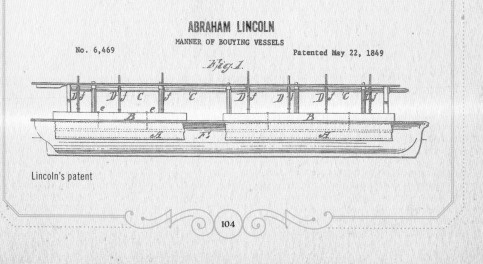

ABRAHAM LINCOLN
MANNER OF BOUYING VESSELS
No. 6,469   Patented May 22, 1849

Lincoln's patent

needed. Worse, Stanton treated Lincoln poorly, writing him off as a hick western lawyer of little value. While angry at being tossed out of what he thought was his case, Lincoln turned it into an educational experience, watching the trial and learning a great deal about how more classically educated eastern lawyers worked a case.[19]

Lincoln was no stranger to patents. In 1849 he received his own patent, the only president before or after to obtain one, for "an improved method of lifting vessels over shoals." Based in part on his own experience getting his flatboat stuck on the New Salem mill dam, and witnessing a steamer stuck on shoals in the Detroit River, Lincoln's invention "combine[d] adjustable buoyant air chambers with a steam boat for the purpose of enabling their draught of water to be readily lessened to enable them to pass over bars, or through shallow water, without discharging their cargoes." He received Patent No. 6469.[20] The system was never put to practical use, but it demonstrated Lincoln's analytical mind and interest in technology, skills that often came into place in his court cases.[21]

Effie Afton Case

That interest in technology came to the fore when Lincoln took on one of the most important cases of his career, which was also critical to America's future. In 1857, Chicago saw the trial of *Hurd v. Rock Island Bridge Company*, better known as the Effie Afton case. The *Effie Afton* was a side-wheeler steamship plying the Mississippi River until it ran into a railroad drawbridge crossing the river from Rock Island, Illinois, to Davenport, Iowa. Within minutes, both the steamship and the bridge caught fire and were destroyed. The captain of the *Effie Afton*, John Hurd, sued the railroad company for obstructing navigation on the river. The railroad company called in Lincoln.

The case was critical because this was the first railroad bridge built across the Mississippi River. It had been opened to rail traffic for only fifteen days before the *Effie Afton* hit it. Prior to the bridge all commercial traffic ran north to south via the river. Railroads were being built at a rapid pace, and the bridge represented the ability to quickly ship commercial wares east to west, which was a major threat to the steamship business. This was the battle of the steamships versus the railroads, with the result hanging on this precedent-setting trial.

Lincoln spent a week on location examining the currents and geography before giving a persuasive closing statement explaining technical aspects to the

FOLLOWING: A slave auction house

jury. As a result, many on the panel were persuaded the bridge was not an obstruction and the crash was caused by operator-error of the steamship's pilot. Officially the trial ended in a hung jury, but in practice it guaranteed that railroad companies could build bridges across the river without fear of being sued as obstructions. Lincoln had set the stage for opening up the West.[22]

Slavery Cases

During his law career Lincoln rarely dealt with slavery cases, but at least two are important to note as interesting contrasts. The first, *Bailey v. Cromwell*, is commonly misrepresented as Lincoln freeing a slave woman named Nance. In reality, Lincoln represented Bailey, who had signed a promissory note to buy Nance, a black slave (or merely "indentured servant"—her exact status was unclear). Bailey refused to pay the note because the seller had not provided documentation confirming her status. Lincoln lost the case in court, but won on appeal in the Illinois Supreme Court, where he argued the Northwest Ordinance of 1787 and Illinois State Constitution presumed that all persons on Illinois soil were free unless proven otherwise. The role of Nance in pressing for her own freedom cannot be underestimated, but Lincoln set a precedent with his unique argument for slave freedom.[23]

The other, known simply as the Matson case, is the only one in which Lincoln ever represented a slave owner. It occurred six years after the Bailey case. Robert Matson was a slave owner who shuttled between his wife and children in Kentucky and his mistress and their four children in Illinois. Matson brought a slave, Jane Bryant, and her children to his farm in Illinois, and when he planned to return them to Kentucky she tried to escape and was caught. After some confusion that almost had him working for Bryant's attorneys, Lincoln ended up representing Matson, arguing that Bryant was only in transit and thus had not met the test required for being domiciled in the state. This seemingly contradicted his earlier argument in the Bailey case, but Lincoln lost and the judge ruled that Jane Bryant and her children were freed. Matson, who was litigious by nature and often refused to pay his bills, never paid Lincoln, and Lincoln never attempted to get payment, perhaps out of relief that he lost.[24]

OLN HAD PLENTY OF WORK, AS IT TURNED OUT!
ARTNERSHIP WITH HIS FORMER POLITICAL
ONENT, STUART, HE OCCUPIED AN OFFICE OF
TS OVER THE CIRCUIT COURTROOM.

... BECAUSE STUART WAS AWAY MOST OF T
ME CAMPAI NING FOR CONGRESS AGAINST TH

LINCOLN TOOK EVERY KIND OF CASE, RANGIN[G]
FROM SUITS FOR DIVORCE, THROUGH PROPE[R]
DEEDS AND BUSINESS DOCUMENTS, TO MURD[ER]
TRIALS. HE HANDLED MOST OF THEM ALONE[.]

TWICE THEY CLINCHED, IN A WELL-MATCH[ED]
ROUGH-AND-TUMBLE - - - TO THE DELIGH[T]
THE CROWD! THE LAST TIME - - - DOUGL[AS]

CHAPTER 6

A HOUSE DIVIDED— SLAVERY ON THE RISE

Lincoln had been out of politics for several years before passage of the Kansas-Nebraska Act in 1854 "aroused him as he had never been before."[1] The Act increased the potential for slavery expansion into the territories. Lincoln was adamantly opposed to this.

It was not Lincoln's first exposure to the slavery question. One reason his family moved to Indiana was to leave Kentucky slavery behind. From an early age Lincoln felt slavery was morally abhorrent. Slavery also made it difficult for white laborers to find jobs in free states. On his two flatboat trips to New Orleans, Lincoln directly encountered slave markets and chain gangs of slaves being transported and sold. These experiences galvanized his distaste for the brutal institution. During his one term as a congressman in Washington, D.C., he lamented the presence of slave pens not far from the steps of the Capitol and drafted a measure that would have banned slavery in the District.

A considerable motivation for Lincoln's opposition to the Mexican War, as expressed in his "spot" resolutions, was that the new territory would increase the spread of slavery. In 1848 he supported the Wilmot Proviso, which would have banned slavery in any territory won from Mexico. It failed to pass. Even his home state of Illinois, which was a constitutionally free state, had restrictive "black laws" that made it difficult for free blacks to reside there. During his years in the state legislature Lincoln led a protest against anti-abolitionist laws that reaffirmed the rights of slave owners, not because he supported slavery—which he believed was "founded on both injustice and bad policy"—but because he thought abolition doctrines made it harder to work with southern states toward the eventual elimination of slavery.[2]

OPPOSITE: *Abe Lincoln Breasting the Winds* by Douglas Volk (1926)

Wilmot

Lincoln loathed slavery as far back as the late 1830s, but he rarely spoke out about the slavery question until the 1850s. There were several reasons for his silence, starting with his belief that the institution was dying out. In a response to Stephen A. Douglas in June 1858, he told a Chicago audience that the Republican Party was made up of people "who will hope for its ultimate extinction."[3] How could it not be so, he thought, given that slavery is morally wrong and politically unsustainable?

This belief proved to be naïve. The invention of the cotton gin in 1793 had made it possible to separate cotton fibers from its seeds mechanically; previously this painstaking process was performed entirely by hand and involved hundreds of hours of manual, usually slave, labor. Most northern states had banned slavery, but southern states saw an expansion of slavery correlated with the growth of "King Cotton." With the separation (ginning) process speeding the rate of production, plantation owners could dramatically increase the acreage on which they grew cotton. As cotton acreage expanded, more and more slaves were needed for cultivation. Rather than being on the cusp of extinction, slavery was booming.[4]

Once he recognized this reality, Lincoln focused on how to stop its expansion. While the words "slavery" and "slave" were intentionally omitted in the Constitution, Article 1, Section 2, Clause 3 tacitly recognized slavery in its "three-fifths of all

ABOVE: The Wilmot Proviso. OPPOSITE: Anti-slavery map, the slave states in black, with gray shading representing its potential spread.

other Persons" clause. Most constitutional scholars of the time agreed that the Constitution protected slavery in the states where it existed, and Lincoln believed that the federal government had no authority to arbitrarily ban slaves in those states. Instead it would be up to the individual states to determine the future of slaves within their borders. This was his main objection to abolitionists, who denied that the Constitution protected slavery and argued the federal government had a fundamental right to ban slavery nationally.

Lincoln did believe, however, that the federal government had an absolute right to block the extension of slavery into the territories, areas in the western United States that had not yet been formally incorporated as states. He based this belief on the Northwest Ordinance, which stipulated that slavery would not be allowed in the northwest region now bounded by Ohio, Indiana, Illinois in the south, and Michigan, Wisconsin, and part of Minnesota in the north. Given that

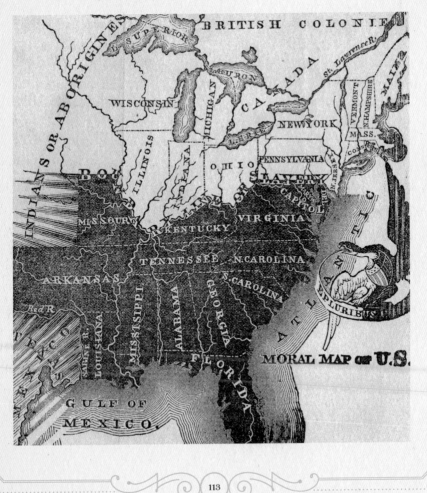

the same Founders who had written the Declaration of Independence where "all men are created equal" and the Constitution had also framed the Northwest Ordinance, he interpreted this as giving authority to the federal government to control the spread of slavery. In 1807 these same Founders also passed an Act banning the importation of slaves from Africa and elsewhere.

Lincoln thought the combined impact of stopping the slave trade and blocking the extension of slavery into the territories would naturally lead to the end of slavery, although he estimated it might take another half-century to accomplish. All that changed with the passage of the Kansas-Nebraska Act.

Kansas-Nebraska Act

After his term in Congress, Lincoln returned to Springfield and focused on his law practice with William Herndon. He still kept up on political news, but was essentially out of politics for several years. As he watched, however, Lincoln grew increasingly worried about the direction in which the slavery issue was taking the country. Failure of the Wilmot Proviso meant there was nothing keeping much of the new territory acquired from Mexico from becoming slave states. The Missouri Compromise of 1820, spearheaded by Henry Clay, blocked any expansion of slavery above the parallel 36°30' north, with the exception of Missouri, which would be admitted as a slave state to balance the number of free and slave states. Whereas the Missouri Compromise had helped avert the civil war that South Carolina and other states were threatening, the Mexican War opened up a huge expanse of new territory below the parallel, potentially increasing the national power of slave states dramatically.

Another important event occurred in 1850: passage of the Fugitive Slave Act. Part of yet another compromise between slave states and free states, the Act further strengthened the enforcement of a Constitutional provision that runaway slaves be returned to their owners. While Article 4, Section 3, Clause 3 of the Constitution is vague on who is responsible for capturing and returning slaves, the Fugitive Slave Act of 1850 made it the explicit responsibility of Federal Marshalls to track down runaway slaves. Anyone assisting slaves in escaping or hiding from capture could be arrested and fined. The law now had teeth. Still, Lincoln did not get involved in this debate because he acknowledged that the Constitution protected the right of slave owners to retrieve escaped slaves.

OPPOSITE: The Kansas-Nebraska Act
FOLLOWING: *A Ride for Liberty—The Fugitive Slaves* by Eastman Johnson (1862)

Thirty-third

Congress of the United States,

At the First Session

BEGUN AND HELD AT THE CITY OF WASHINGTON

in the District of Columbia

on Monday the fifth day of December one thousand eight hundred and fifty-three.

AN ACT To organize the Territories of Nebraska and Kansas.

Be It Enacted by the Senate and House of Representatives of the United States of America in Congress assembled,

That all that part of the Territory of the United States included within the following limits, except such portions thereof as are herein-after expressly exempted from the operations of this act, to-wit: beginning at a point in the Missouri river where the fortieth parallel of north latitude crosses the same; thence west on said parallel to the east boundary of the Territory of Utah, on the summit of the Rocky Mountains; thence on said summit northward to the forty-ninth parallel of north latitude; thence east on said parallel to the western boundary of the Territory of Minnesota; thence southward on said boundary to the Missouri river; thence down the main channel of said river to the place of beginning, and the same is hereby, created into a temporary government by the name of the Territory of Nebraska; and when admitted as a State or States, the said Territory, or any portion of the same, shall be received into the Union with or without slavery, as their constitution may prescribe at the time of their admission: Provided, That nothing in this act contained shall be construed to inhibit the government of the United States from dividing said Territory into two or more Territories, in such manner and at such times as Congress shall deem convenient and proper, or from attaching any portion of said Territory to any other State or Territory of the United States: Provided further, That nothing in this act contained shall be construed to impair the rights of person or property now pertaining

But then came 1854 and the Kansas-Nebraska Act, introduced in January by Democratic rival Stephen A. Douglas. Aside from creating the new territories of

Kansas and Nebraska, the Act repealed the long-standing Missouri Compromise that limited slavery below the designated parallel. Now territories would be allowed to decide for themselves whether they would allow slavery, a right that Douglas called Popular Sovereignty.

Lincoln was livid. This meant slavery could potentially extend throughout the newly expanded western territories as they were admitted into the Union. Slavery was not slowly devolving into extinction; rather, the opposite was happening—it was spreading across America. In contrast, Douglas argued that his Popular Sovereignty was inherently American; the great principle of self-government was at stake. Of course, he meant self-government of the white population, given that black slaves had no say in whether they were brought into the new territories.

In practice, the decision-making process was not as easy as Douglas led everyone to believe. Given that the voting on whether to be formed as a free or a slave state required establishment of a requisite population, a mass migration of citizens from other states was needed. Both pro- and anti-slavery elements raced to populate the Kansas territory in order to sway the voting. Abolitionists like William Lloyd Garrison and other promi-nent members of the American Anti-Slavery Society (including Frederick Douglass) helped raise awareness and funds for people who wanted to migrate west. Pro-slavery factions, especially from the South, also raced to saturate the land with people who would vote for legal slavery. The battles between these two groups turned

TOP: Stephen A. Douglas. ABOVE: William Lloyd Garrison.
OPPOSITE: Currier & Ives satirical cartooon about "Bleeding Kansas"

violent, leading to a protracted period of upheaval known as "Bleeding Kansas," which lasted from 1854 until the onset of the Civil War.

Two incidents illustrated the tensions that the expansion of slavery caused. In May 1856, John Brown and a band of abolitionists massacred five settlers north of Pottawatomie Creek in Kansas. Their actions were in retaliation for pro-slavery forces who had ransacked the town of Lawrence, Kansas, which anti-slavery settlers established to ensure Kansas would become a free state. (John Brown also led a failed attempt to start a slave rebellion at Harpers Ferry in 1859.)

The second incident occurred in Washington two days before the Pottawatomie massacre. Senator Charles Sumner of Massachusetts, a staunch abolitionist, gave a speech in which he fiercely attacked the Kansas-Nebraska Act and its primary authors, Stephen A. Douglas of Illinois and Andrew Butler of South Carolina. Preston Brooks, a representative from South Carolina and cousin to Butler, took offense. He walked calmly into the Senate chambers, then beat Sumner repeatedly with his heavy gold-headed cane while two allies kept other senators from stopping the attack. His legs trapped under the small Senate desk, Sumner was so severely injured it was three years before he returned to full duties in the Senate. Slavery was once again the main issue driving politics in America.

THE "FIRST SCALP", TAKEN IN THE KANSAS WAR.

Peoria

As the Kansas-Nebraska Act was renewing Lincoln's interest in politics, his Whig Party was coming to an end. The party had weakened and fragmented when Whig leaders such as Henry Clay and Daniel Webster died in 1852. Southern Whigs supported the Kansas-Nebraska Act because it allowed the expansion of slavery, while Northern Whigs strongly opposed it. This North-South split mirrored the divided Democratic Party in 1860, but in 1854 southerners generally shifted to the Democratic Party or joined the new American Party. The latter were also known as the Know-Nothings because of their secrecy and nativist bigotry against blacks, as well as Irish and Catholic immigrants. Former northern Whigs, including Lincoln, along with anti-slavery Democrats, formed a new Republican party. The Republican Party's primary focus was to prevent the expansion of slavery into the territories.

In October 1854 Lincoln rose to the forefront of the Republicans with a speech he gave first in Springfield, and then a dozen days later in Peoria. Newspapers published the second presentation, so it came to be known as the Peoria speech. It began when Stephen A. Douglas, the originator of the Kansas-Nebraska policy, spoke to a large crowd at the state fair in Springfield. Lincoln was in the audience and proclaimed that he would respond to Douglas's arguments, saying "Douglas lied; he lied three times and I'll prove it!"[5] That afternoon he did so at the Illinois state house. While Lincoln sat quietly listening to Douglas's speech, Douglas repeatedly interrupted Lincoln.[6]

Lincoln vigorously condemned slavery. After giving a brief history of slavery in America, he denounced it. He reiterated his belief that slavery was morally and politically wrong, but also that the Constitution protected it in the areas where it already existed. Therefore, the federal government could not remove it from the South, but it could, and must, restrict its spread into the territories. The Kansas-Nebraska Act, he argued, violated those principles, and Douglas was contradicting himself with regard to his support for the Missouri Compromise, which the Act now voided. Lincoln made his views on the Kansas-Nebraska Act clear:

> I cannot but hate. I hate it because of the monstrous injustice of slavery itself. I hate it because it deprives our republican example of its just influence in the world—enables the enemies of free institutions, with plausibility, to taunt us as hypocrites—causes the real friends of freedom to doubt our sincerity, and especially because it forces so many really good men amongst ourselves into an open war with the very

principles of civil liberty—criticizing the Declaration of Independence, and insisting that there is no right principle of action but self-interest.[7]

Lincoln further argued that slaves and free blacks were men, and as such had the same right to self-governance that white men did. Quoting from the Declaration of Independence, Lincoln asserted that the phrase "all men are created equal" included black men as well as white, and that "no man is good enough to govern another man, without that other's consent."[8]

These were progressive words in 1854. Being anti-slavery in the North did not necessarily signify belief in equality between the races. Lincoln recognized that even if all slaves were free, society would not function given inherent inequalities, attitudes, and bigotries. Overlooking the fact that most slaves at this time had been born in America, he favored colonization as a means for free blacks to leave the United States and set up black-led countries of their own. Despite this inconsistency, by forcefully arguing for the moral wrong of slavery and the dangers of slavery spreading because of the Kansas-Nebraska Act, Lincoln set the framework for a slavery debate that lasted the rest of the decade.

A House Divided Cannot Stand

The new Republican Party nominated John C. Fremont for president in 1856, but because the former Whig vote was split between Republicans and the Know-Nothings, Democrat James Buchanan was elected president. That same year Lincoln lost his race for a Senate seat. The following spring, days after Buchanan's inauguration, Supreme Court Chief Justice Roger Taney issued the Dred Scott decision. Scott was a slave whose owner had lived many years in Illinois (a free state) and Wisconsin (a free territory). Scott tried unsuccessfully to buy his freedom, then sued for release based on his long residency in free states, where the Northwest Ordinance made slavery illegal. After the case reached the Supreme Court, Chief Justice Taney wrote the majority decision in a substantially pro-slavery Court (five of nine justices were from the South and another was outspoken in his pro-slavery views). Going beyond established precedent and attributing to the Founders beliefs that were not supported by fact, Taney declared that Scott was not only not considered free despite his residence in free states, he was not to be even considered a person under the U.S. Constitution. Taney argued that slaves and their descendants could never be citizens, and would always remain the property of their owners.

7

DRED SCOTT

Lincoln quickly understood the two great ramifications of this decision (in addition to the obvious result of Scott's family being forced back into slavery). First, the decision endangered *all* blacks, including those who had been born free or achieved their freedom by owner emancipation or self-purchase. Second, it revealed a dramatic contradiction in Douglas's Popular Sovereignty scheme. Lincoln later exploited that contradiction and placed Douglas in a compromising position during the Lincoln-Douglas debates—a position from which Douglas would not be able to extract himself.

In 1858 Lincoln had another opportunity to run for Senate, this time against his old rival Stephen A. Douglas. In June Lincoln gave what is perhaps one of his most cited oratories, the "House Divided" speech. Once again he warned that the Kansas-Nebraska Act had opened the country to expansion of slavery—not just in the territories, but throughout the nation. Beginning with a paraphrased line from the Bible (Mark 3:25), Lincoln notes:

> *A house divided against itself cannot stand. I believe this government cannot endure, permanently, half slave and half free. I do not expect the Union to be dissolved—I do not expect the house to fall—but I do expect it will cease to be divided. It will become all one thing or all the other. Either the opponents of slavery will arrest the further spread of it, and place it where the public mind shall rest in the belief it is in the course of ultimate extinction; or its advocates will push it forward, till it shall become lawful in all the states, old as well as new—North as well as South.*[9]

Lincoln was not using hyperbole; he firmly believed slavery was in danger of becoming a national institution. The Kansas-Nebraska Act could allow all of the remaining territories to welcome slavery. The Fugitive Slave Act required the federal government and all states to actively capture any slaves who had escaped into free states and return them to the South. And the Dred Scott decision had effectively invalidated any rights of citizenship even for free blacks, no matter where they lived. One more Supreme Court decision like Dred Scott could result in the right of slave owners to move to any free state and legally bring their slaves, thus making all of the United States open to slavery.

The night before giving his speech, Lincoln asked Republican friends to read it and offer advice. Unanimously they begged him to tone down the passage cited

OPPOSITE: Portrait of Dred Scott

REPORT

OF

THE DECISION

OF THE

Supreme Court of the United States,

AND THE

OPINIONS OF THE JUDGES THEREOF,

IN THE CASE OF

DRED SCOTT

VERSUS

JOHN F. A. SANDFORD.

DECEMBER TERM, 1856.

BY BENJAMIN C. HOWARD,
FROM THE NINETEENTH VOLUME OF HOWARD'S REPORTS

WASHINGTON:
CORNELIUS WENDELL, PRINTER.
1857.

above, fearing it was too inflammatory. Lincoln listened, and then told them he would keep it in: "I think the time has come to say it, and I will let it go as is."[10] Those who felt slavery was wrong had been compromising for decades, with all compromises resulting in continued political strength to slave owners. For Lincoln, the time had come to make a stand.

Lincoln–Douglas Debates

After his "House Divided" speech, Lincoln began following Douglas from town to town as they campaigned against each other. As the incumbent senator in a Democrat-dominated state, Lincoln had to coax Douglas to go against his own interests and formally debate. Whenever Douglas gave a major speech, Lincoln told the crowd he would respond that evening or the next day. After doing this for a while, and with the help of his influential friend Jesse Fell, Lincoln approached Douglas about holding a series of joint debates across the state. Reluctant at first, Douglas eventually agreed to one debate in each of the nine congressional districts in Illinois. They had both already spoken in Springfield and Chicago within a day of each other, so they agreed to seven additional joint debates in Ottawa, Freeport, Jonesboro, Charleston, Galesburg, Quincy, and Alton over the next two months. For each debate one candidate would speak for sixty minutes, followed by the other for ninety minutes, and the first would get a thirty-minute reply. They alternated who would speak first, with the incumbent Douglas getting the benefit of doing so in four of the seven debates.[11]

The optics of the debates were almost comical. Lincoln was as tall and thin as Douglas was short and wide. Douglas tended toward inflammatory and racist language, while Lincoln was calmer and more logical in his arguments. Douglas had a reputation as a blatant liar; Lincoln as "Honest Abe." Douglas often arrived in town on a special train accompanied by boisterous bands. Lincoln rode coach. Douglas was prone to histrionics, personal attacks, dogmatic exclamations, blatantly negrophobic pandering to white superiority, and lying without remorse. Lincoln avoided sliding in the muck, focusing on making his key points clear to the often large crowds.[12]

Because of the way Illinois was settled—its southern section filled with people from slave states, the central with free-state Easterners, and the north with people from the Great Lakes region—each debate city offered a different range of

OPPOSITE: Summary of the Dred Scott case

public opinion. While topics like banking were briefly mentioned, the main focus of all debates was the defining issue of the day—slavery.

Douglas and Lincoln explored several aspects of the slavery question, with Douglas largely sticking to his stump speech at each stop while Lincoln built on his arguments over time. One aspect was whether slavery was right or wrong. Lincoln argued that slavery was inherently wrong, both from a moral view and from a public policy perspective. Douglas, who asserted that he "cares not whether slavery is voted down or voted up,"[13] believed that a state could choose whether it wanted slavery, and the federal government had no right to dictate policy. Lincoln disagreed, noting again that the Founders had banned slavery from the territories that became Ohio, Indiana, Illinois, and parts north. The Founders also banned the import of new slaves from Africa. As such, Lincoln argued, the federal government had every right to restrict slavery in the territories, and had done so repeatedly.

Sensing this was a difficult position, Douglas went on the attack. He accused Lincoln and all "Black Republicans" of being abolitionists, intent on removing slavery from all the southern states where it currently existed. Lincoln denied this, reminding people that he acknowledged the Constitution protected slavery where it existed. His goal was simply to stop it from expanding. Douglas took his attacks a step further, accusing Lincoln of being for the full equality of the races. Again Lincoln denied this, saying in the Charleston debate:

> *I am not, nor ever have been, in favor of bringing about in any way the social and political equality of the white and black races, that I am not nor ever have been in favor of making voters or jurors of negroes, nor of qualifying them to hold office, nor to intermarry with white people.*

Clarifying further, he noted:

> *I do not understand that because I do not want a negro woman for a slave I must necessarily want her for a wife. My understanding is that I can just let her alone.*[14]

Whether Lincoln was expressing his own racial views or carefully wording his response to the overtly prejudicial crowds is uncertain. In any case, he quickly moved on to the issue he had been planning for some time.

OPPOSITE: The Lincoln–Douglas debates

In the first debate in Ottawa, Douglas had asked Lincoln seven questions. Lincoln waited until the second debate in Freeport to address them, and by then had worked up a set of four questions of his own to posit to Douglas. Always thinking ahead, Lincoln set a trap, and Douglas had no choice but to fall into what would become known as the Freeport Doctrine. Lincoln asked:

> *Can the people of a United States Territory, in any lawful way, against the wish of any citizen of the United States, exclude slavery from its limits prior to the formation of a State Constitution?*[15]

The question pitted Douglas's Popular Sovereignty against the Supreme Court's Dred Scott decision. Douglas was forced to choose between alienating those people he needed to get reelected to the Illinois Senate or the Southerners he needed in his third run for the presidency two years later. He responded that people in a territory could keep out slavery despite the Dred Scott decision, which stated that federal and state governments had no authority to exclude slavery because it would deprive slaveholders of their "property" rights without due process.

Lincoln was ecstatic over Douglas's response, although he did not show his hand. Southerners, who wanted to expand slavery without limit, had grown concerned

"TAKING THE STUMP" OR STEPHEN IN SEARCH OF HIS MOTHER.

Published by Currier & Ives, 194 Nassau St. N.Y.

that states could exclude slavery in accordance with Douglas's Popular Sovereignty. They saw the Dred Scott decision as confirming their right to bring slaves wherever they wanted, and now Douglas was saying that was not true. This presented a long-term problem for slave-owning states. While they knew that most of the new territories were grossly inadequate for growing cotton, which was still the primary driver of the need for slaves, they recognized that every new slave state would increase their representation in Congress—and their continued power to dictate policy.

When the votes were counted, Lincoln had won the popular vote and the Republican Party picked up seats in the legislature. But the state legislature, which was majority Democratic, was still choosing senators. Douglas retained his Senate seat. Lincoln likely realized his chances of winning the seat were close to nil because of the legislature's makeup. When he was asked why he would give Douglas an advantage for Senate reelection, Lincoln replied that he had a longer view in mind: Douglas might win the Senate, but he would lose the presidency. The Freeport Doctrine would see to that.

OPPOSITE: 1860 Currier & Ives political cartoon with Lincoln, Douglas, and the other 1860 candidates. Douglas is hobbled, on a crutch and begging for coins, while the others lampoon him with witty remarks.

 H ANGERED BY THE ELECTION RESULT,
COLN WAS BY NO MEANS DISCOURAGED!
ONG BELIEVED THAT ONE DAY HER
WOULD BE PRESIDENT.

THEY STRETCHED A STRING WHICH TOOK
N'S TOPPER OFF, AND THERE WAS A RAIN
TTERS, NOTES AND WHAT

E NEIGHBORHOOD SMALL BOYS, NOT CONCE
TH MR. LINCOLN'S POLITICAL FUTURE, LOC
HIM AS AN OLD FRIEND --- ONE ON WHOM IT
AFE TO PLAY JOKES.

AS HE GOT DOWN TO COLLECT THE PAPERS
SWARMED OVER HIM IN PRETENDED ATTAC
ING AND LAUGHING. AND LINCOLN LAUGHE
LOVING EVERY YOUNG SCAMP.

CHAPTER 7

RUNNING FOR PRESIDENT

Newspapers eagerly covered the Lincoln–Douglas debates, with reporters desperately trying to write down three hours of speeches in a noisy outdoor venue without volume amplification. Douglas's voice did not carry quite as well as Lincoln's, and much of what both said was hard to hear, especially at the sites drawing tens of thousands of people. Reporters sometimes paraphrased or even left out parts they did not hear clearly. Worse, newspapers were highly partisan. Democratic papers cleaned up Douglas's speechifying so it was grammatically correct and persuasive while printing Lincoln's speeches as they were spoken, or even garbled to make him seem unintelligible. The Republican papers likewise accentuated Lincoln and debased Douglas.

Seeing the value of the published debates, Lincoln took matters into his own hands and constructed a scrapbook. To ensure fairness, he retrieved Douglas's portions from Democratic newspapers and his own speeches from Republican ones. The book with all seven of the debates was published in early 1860. It became a bestseller, and made clear to everyone the positions of Douglas and Lincoln on the key question of the day.

Likely not long after Lincoln lost the 1858 Senate race, he began to think of himself as a potential presidential candidate. Mary had been putting the idea in his head for some time, so when his friend Jesse Fell insisted that Lincoln was more electable than other Republican leaders, including New York Senator William Seward and Ohio Governor Salmon P. Chase, Lincoln relented: "I admit that I am ambitious, and would like to be President." Lincoln felt that Seward and Chase might have had a greater right to the nomination than he did, but he had received 110 votes in a second-place finish for the vice presidential nomination in 1856, and he had fewer enemies (and voting records) than the others. As he analyzed the situation he had to agree that Fell was right; his chances for election appeared to be significant.[1]

OPPOSITE: *Abraham Lincoln* by N. C. Wyeth (1938)

Determining the Preferred Characteristics

Lincoln spent 1859 tending to his law practice in order to replenish his financial reserves. Business had diminished sharply during the Senate campaign, and Lincoln had to pay the bills. But he also kept in touch with party business during this time, giving political speeches in Illinois, Indiana, and Kansas and writing letters to other party leaders. His goals were twofold: first, retain his profile among potential voters and party insiders; second, help define the Republican Party as the middle ground between the extremes of radical abolition and Douglas's Popular Sovereignty.

This middle ground was key to Lincoln's chances. Seward and Chase were considered too radical, limiting their chances of capturing the swing states. Lincoln reminded everyone that he was not an abolitionist; he believed the Constitution protected slavery where it existed in the South. But he was not going to compromise on his position that the federal government had a right to block the spread of slavery into the territories.

Harpers Ferry insurrectionists inside engine house just before gate is broken down

Although neither Seward nor Lincoln was in any way connected with John Brown, the abolitionist's raid at Harpers Ferry in October 1859 had a fundamental impact on their chances for the nomination. Brown had already made headlines for his role in the Pottawatomie massacre during Bleeding Kansas, and now he was attempting to start a slave revolt in western Virginia. Leading twenty-one poorly trained men, Brown attacked a federal arsenal in hopes of getting weapons for the revolt. It did not go well. His expectation that hundreds of escaped slaves would join his band went unheeded, and within days his band was defeated by U.S. Marines under the command of (then still loyally Union) Colonel Robert E. Lee. After a brief trial, Brown was sentenced to death and hanged.

The raid increased already rampant paranoia in the South, which firmly believed the North was intent on abolishing slavery throughout the nation. Caught in the crosshairs of this anguish was William Seward, considered a radical of the Republican Party because of his "irrepressible conflict" and "higher authority" speeches, which many interpreted as his belief that civil war was inevitable. Lincoln's "House Divided" speech also could have been interpreted that way, but because his language and demeanor were less threatening (and because he was much less well known), he was not labeled a radical. The John Brown raid also spooked northern political leaders, who feared that if they nominated someone like Seward they might not win the election.

Horace Greeley, the highly influential editor of the New York *Tribune*, also believed the raid "will probably help us to nominate a moderate man for Pres[iden]t." He described the perfect Republican candidate:

> [An] anti-slavery man per se cannot be elected; but a Tariff, River-and-Harbor, Pacific Railroad, Free-Homestead man may succeed although he is anti-slavery.[2]

Greeley was describing his favored candidate at the time, Edward Bates, an aging former congressman and attorney general from Missouri. Some considered Bates a viable presidential candidate, but many in the Republican Party felt he was overly conservative, tainted by his association with the nativist Know-Nothings, and not particularly dynamic as a leader. Unbeknownst to Greeley, the characteristics he described also fit Abraham Lincoln—without all the negatives.

FOLLOWING: This painting illustrates a sensationalized newspaper account of John Brown stopping to kiss a baby on his way to being hanged.

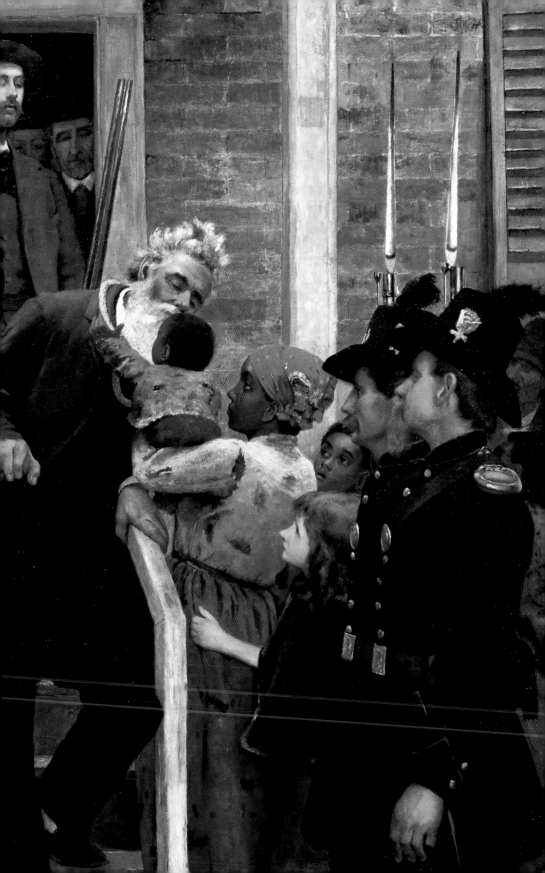

Cooper Union

In the fall of 1859, Republican wins in state elections in Ohio, Pennsylvania, Iowa, and Minnesota hurt Douglas's chances to get the nomination at the 1860 Democratic convention in Charleston, South Carolina.[3] Seeing his own prospects improving, Lincoln wrote letters to key party influencers to keep them focused on the main issue of the day—stopping the expansion of slavery into the territories. He warned them not to veer into side debates on the tariff or the Fugitive Slave Act, two issues that were important regionally but on which there was no unanimous support in the states Republicans would need for the presidential election. At the urging of Jesse Fell, in December 1859 Lincoln provided a short "anonymous" autobiography to be used for an article introducing him to eastern voters.

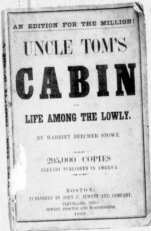

Published on February 11, 1860, with additional annotation by Joseph Lewis in the *Chester County Times*, the profile was widely copied in other Republican papers as an introduction to Lincoln. Showing his wry sense of humor and understanding of how the issue was perceived, Lincoln ended his anonymous piece with a physical description of himself. To emphasize the slavery issue, he structured it in the form seen in newspaper advertising demanding the capture of runaway slaves:

> *If any personal description of me is thought desirable, it may be said, I am, in height, six feet, four inches, nearly; lean in flesh, weighing, on the average, one hundred and eighty pounds; dark complexion, with coarse black hair, and grey eyes—no other marks or brands recollected.*[4]

Lincoln tried to keep a low profile to avoid attracting unwanted attention, publicly suggesting that while he was flattered to be considered, he might not be on a par with the more visible Republican leaders. At the same time, he continued to work with his allies to position himself as a viable candidate if the opportunity arose. When he received an invitation to give a lecture at Plymouth Church in Brooklyn, home of Henry Ward Beecher, he accepted with the stipulation that he could address a political topic.[5]

ABOVE: First edition of *Uncle Tom's Cabin*.   OPPOSITE: Henry Ward Beecher.

Beecher came from an activist family that included his sister Harriet Beecher Stowe, author of the highly controversial and wildly successful novel *Uncle Tom's Cabin*. As a clergyman, social reformer, and staunch abolitionist, Beecher was decidedly influential in political circles. Originally Lincoln was slated to be the final speaker in a series of speeches sponsored by the Plymouth Church, but he could not make the trip until after the series ended. The sponsorship was eventually turned over to the Young Men's Republican Union of New York, whose advisors included anti-Seward men such as Greeley and William Cullen Bryant. Lincoln was invited because the sponsors were looking for an alternative to Seward in the forthcoming nomination battle.

Lincoln conducted an immense amount of research to develop his lecture. But when he arrived in New York in February 1860 he discovered the venue had been changed from Beecher's Brooklyn church to the Cooper Union for the Advancement of Science and Art in lower Manhattan. Fearing his planned lecture would be insufficient for the more educated crowd expected at Cooper Union, Lincoln spent the night before making last-minute revisions. That morning he took time to be photographed by Mathew Brady, a side trip that would prove immensely beneficial in the next few months as people scrambled to get a look at this western unknown. On the evening of the speech he felt somewhat lacking in comparison to the august company on the stage. When he began to speak, his Kentucky-born drawl and high-pitched voice came out with "Mr. Cheerman."

Once he warmed up, however, he drew in the crowd and kept them engrossed for the next ninety minutes with an intensely systematic walk through the support for federal authority to restrict slavery. The speech is dry and logical compared with his better-known Gettysburg Address and Inaugural Addresses, but it was direct and effective. It had three main parts.

The first part dealt with the question of the extension of slavery, as raised by Stephen A. Douglas in an article published the previous fall in which he suggested:

> *Our fathers, when they framed the Government under which we live,*
> *understood this question just as well, and even better, than we do now.*[6]

Douglas was here insinuating that the Founders had settled the question of expansion by including the concept, if not the words, of slavery in the Constitution. Lincoln, repeating Douglas's words several times in mockery, diligently and systematically showed how the men who framed the Constitution had repeatedly voted in favor of federal government authority to restrict slavery in the territories. To Lincoln, there was absolute proof that "our fathers" not only understood the question, but also clearly and intentionally put slavery on the track toward its ultimate extinction.

The second part of the speech was directed at southerners, "if they will listen—as I suppose they will not." He asked southerners for patience, yet also noted that if they sought disunion, it would be because of their own actions, not any action on the part of the North.[7]

In the final section Lincoln returned attention to his fellow Republicans, urging them never to abandon the principles unnerving the South, ending with a tremendously powerful peroration:

> Neither let us be slandered from our duty by false accusations against us, nor frightened from it by menaces of destruction to the Government nor of dungeons to ourselves. LET US HAVE FAITH THAT RIGHT MAKES RIGHT, AND IN THAT FAITH, LET US, TO THE END, DARE TO DO OUR DUTY AS WE UNDERSTAND IT.[8]

The crowd at Cooper Union went wild, and Lincoln knew he had made a grand impression. He was immediately besieged with requests to repeat his speech on a tour through New England. He had already planned to visit Robert at Phillips Exeter Academy in New Hampshire, so agreed to add a series of ten speeches in

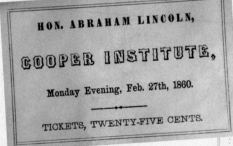

HON. ABRAHAM LINCOLN,

COOPER INSTITUTE,

Monday Evening, Feb. 27th, 1860.

TICKETS, TWENTY-FIVE CENTS.

Rhode Island, New Hampshire, and Connecticut. Mostly he adhered to the basic arguments of his Cooper Union speech, but he also worked in discussions of issues important to the various locales. In Connecticut, for example, he commended the ability of laborers to strike if they wanted, warning that if slavery spread, white workers would lose jobs to black laborers who could not strike. He also touted the ability of free labor to allow even the humblest man an equal chance to get rich if he could manage it, adding that he believed "a black man is entitled" to that same chance to better his condition.

The two-week tour through three New England states allowed Lincoln to present his views on the slavery and free labor questions. Most people were impressed. One professor of rhetoric at Yale lectured his class on the merits of Lincoln's speech, to which one of his students from the South agreed, noting: "That fellow could shut up old Euclid himself, to say nothing of Steve Douglas."[9] This tour was critically important to Lincoln's campaign, as it gave New England voters a chance to see and hear about this intriguing "country lawyer" and politician from the West.

Illinois State
Republican Convention

Lincoln returned from his extended trip both exhausted and exhilarated at his potential in the upcoming presidential election. Hoping for a respite in Illinois, he instead walked into some intraparty bickering among old allies Norman Judd, John Wentworth, Leonard Swett, David Davis, and William Herndon. Carefully maneuvering around egos for the next several weeks, Lincoln also had to manage the various powers that wanted him for vice president in 1860, as well as for governor and Senate. Lincoln wrote many letters and had many conversations in an effort to

OPPOSITE: Lincoln's speech at Cooper Union.   ABOVE: Ticket to the Cooper Union speech.

avoid getting pigeonholed into other offices while delicately expressing his own interest in the presidency. He did all this while also trying to make some money in his much-neglected law practice.

The careful maintenance of these friendships came in handy. After an earlier correspondence with Norman Judd, Lincoln received the unequivocal endorsement of the Chicago *Press and Tribune*, influenced by Judd. In April, Judd wrote to Lyman Trumbull suggesting he promote Lincoln, but avoid getting into battles with other major candidates such as Seward, Chase, Bates, and Simon Cameron. The goal was to remain inconspicuous and let the other candidates fight among themselves so no one would hesitate to turn to Lincoln at the proper time if their own candidate faltered.[10]

It was necessary, however, to get the unanimous support of the Illinois delegation. The Illinois State Republican Convention was held on May 9–10 in Decatur. Having the ostensible purpose of choosing a candidate for Governor and deciding on a platform, the convention also presented an opportunity for Lincoln's allies to gauge support for his presidential candidacy. Among the almost 650 delegates were some who liked Seward and many who supported nearby Missouri's Edward Bates. Lincoln was there as a delegate himself.

Early on the first day, Richard Oglesby, an influential party leader and future three-term governor, made a grandiose gesture of inviting "distinguished citizen" Abraham Lincoln to sit on the speakers platform. Lincoln was idling near the back of the room and could not get through the crowd, so the masses picked him up and passed him "kicking scrambling—crawling—upon the sea of heads between him and the Stand." Lincoln was placed on the platform, bowing in thanks for the unexpected and rather harrowing ride.[11]

After some party business, Oglesby once again rose up and announced another special guest, Lincoln's second cousin John Hanks. Entering in grand style, Hanks and another man carried two wooden fence rails with a placard identifying them as a pair from more than 3,000 rails Hanks and Lincoln made in 1830. The crowd erupted in cheers for Abraham Lincoln. The ever-affable Lincoln, who may or may not have known about the stunt ahead of time, playfully said he did not know for sure whether he split those particular rails, "but whether they were or were not, he had mauled many and many better ones since he had grown to manhood." No matter what the case, Lincoln's nickname "The Rail-Splitter" began that day, and he was forever proud at his skill with an axe.

ABOVE: Richard Oglesby

The stunt was effective. Republicans in the state agreed to unanimously support Lincoln and only Lincoln in the upcoming Republican National Convention in Chicago. Old friend and circuit judge David Davis was named Lincoln's campaign manager, with Norman Judd, Gustav Koerner, and Orville H. Browning named the other at-large delegates.

Republican National Convention in Chicago

Lincoln's preparation for the Republican National Convention actually began in the fall of 1859, with old friend Norman Judd serving on the committee to decide when and where to have the assembly. Each of the main contenders for the nomination wanted a site that best benefitted him: New York's William Seward wanted New York City, Ohioan Salmon P. Chase wanted Cleveland, and Missouri's Edward Bates wanted St. Louis. Judd suggested Chicago. After all, he explained, there was no prominent candidate from Illinois, so Chicago would be a neutral site. The committee agreed to have the convention in Chicago, demonstrating how little they considered Lincoln a viable candidate.[12]

There was one problem: Chicago did not have a building big enough to handle all the delegates, so the national committee allocated funds for building a suitable temporary space. In a credit to engineering, the hastily erected convention hall—nicknamed the Wigwam—provided seating space for more than 10,000 delegates and observers, all with good views of the speaker's platform and excellent acoustics.

As was the custom, Lincoln stayed at home in Springfield while David Davis and a cadre of others who knew Lincoln from the Eighth Judicial Circuit took the train to Chicago. Their strategy was to stop the default support for William Seward, then line up around 100 delegates willing to vote for Lincoln on the first ballot, make sure he gained votes on the second ballot, and win the nomination on the third ballot. For two days before the voting began, Davis and his colleagues talked with delegations from Indiana, Pennsylvania, Ohio, and Massachusetts to encourage them to fall to Lincoln if their preferred candidate failed to get enough support. Lincoln's team was coached to talk about Lincoln's life, character, and great ability. They were instructed to always commend Seward in the highest

FOLLOWING: Republican National Convention of 1860

terms, but point out that he would have difficulty winning the swing states. In stark contrast, Thurlow Weed and other Seward men put on airs of inevitability and put off delegates by telling everyone Lincoln was "greatly the inferior."[13]

In a letter to Samuel Galloway, Lincoln instructed his campaign committee to consider:

> *My name is new in the field; and I suppose I am not the first choice*
> *of a very great many. Our policy, then, is to give no offence to others—*
> *leave them in a mood to come to us, if they shall be compelled to give*
> *up their first love.*[14]

The strategy worked. As expected, Seward received 173.5 votes on the first ballot. Lincoln surprised many by receiving 102, while Cameron, Chase, and Bates attracting only around 50 apiece. On the second ballot, Seward picked up a few votes to 184.5 while Lincoln surged up to 181 as he siphoned votes from the others. After the third ballot Lincoln took the lead with 231.5 out of the 233 needed, with Seward decreasing slightly to 180 and the others falling completely out of contention. Seeing how close Lincoln was, the Ohio delegation switched four votes to give Lincoln enough for the win, further supplemented by a huge wave of changed votes to total 364. Abraham Lincoln was the Republican nominee for President. Hannibal Hamlin of Maine was selected by the delegations as Lincoln's running mate.

The 1860 Election

As expected, northern Democrats nominated Stephen A. Douglas. Because of Lincoln's clever positioning on slavery during the 1858 Lincoln–Douglas debates—especially coaxing Douglas into the Freeport Doctrine—the Democratic Party had split into two factions, and Douglas represented only the North. Southern Democrats from the eleven slave states nominated their own candidate, John C. Breckinridge, the sitting Vice President under James Buchanan. To split the vote further, John Bell was nominated for a new Constitutional Union party, the main goal of which was that everyone just get along.

Lincoln again stayed in Springfield, as it was considered inappropriate for candidates to personally hit the campaign trail. Instead, Seward, Davis, and others

OPPOSITE: Lincoln–Hamlin campaign poster

ON. ABRAHAM LINCOLN, OF ILLINOIS.   HON. HANNIBAL HAMLIN, OF MAINE,

FOR PRESIDENT.   FOR VICE PRESIDENT.

made the case for him. Stephen A. Douglas, in contrast, campaigned extensively, spending a large amount of time in the South warning against disunion. Douglas race-baited as usual, insisting that government was "made by white men for white men" forever, but did try to convince southerners that they were better off working within the Union than trying to separate.[15]

Because the Democratic Party had split, Republicans felt confident that Lincoln would win the election. Indeed, he won with about 40 percent of the popular vote and 180 of the 303 electoral votes available; 152 were needed to win. He won all the northern states plus the two new states of California and Oregon. John Breckinridge came in second, gaining 72 electoral votes from most of the southern slave states. Bell got 39 electoral votes by capturing the three border slave states of Virginia, Kentucky, and Tennessee. Douglas, once considered the likely winner, received only 12 electoral votes from the two states of Missouri and New Jersey. Lincoln was president-elect.

The Rail-Splitter Rides the Rails to Washington

Following the election, Lincoln spent the next several months working out of the Governor's office in the Illinois State House preparing for his trip to Washington. The burdens of answering the many letters he received led to the hiring of John G. Nicolay as personal secretary, and then John Hay to help him when the workload expanded even further. Lincoln also had to decide whom he would invite into his cabinet, with many spirited rivals under consideration. The inauguration was not until March 4, 1861, a full five months after the election, but before he knew it the day had arrived to start the trip.

Climbing aboard the train at the Great Western Depot in Springfield on a cold, rainy day, Lincoln turned to the assembled well-wishers to give a farewell address. Noting he had lived in Springfield for "a quarter of a century," he presciently added "I now leave, not knowing when, or whether ever, I may return, with a task before me greater than that which rested upon Washington."[16] His ten-day train travel took him from Illinois through Indiana, Ohio, New York, Pennsylvania, and Maryland. As he arrived in Philadelphia he was told of an assassination plot against him. Speaking in famed Independence Hall,

OPPOSITE: Lincoln leaving Springfield for Washington, D.C.

Lincoln noted that all his feelings sprung from "the sentiments embodied in the Declaration of Independence" and that if the country could not be saved without giving up on those principles, "I would rather be assassinated on this spot than surrender it."[17]

No assassination attempt materialized at that time, but whether it was thwarted or imagined, Lincoln made the remaining trip through Baltimore and into Washington under cover of night and slightly disguised. These evasive tactics embarrassed him, but he had bigger problems waiting for him—even before the inauguration.

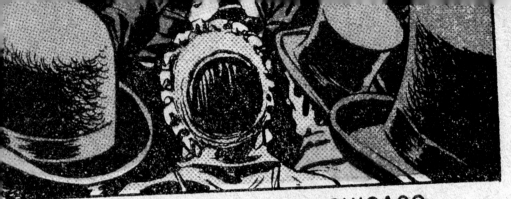

...PUBLICAN CONVENTION IN CHICAGO,
...COLN'S NAME WAS PROPOSED, FIVE THOU-
...CES ROSE IN WILD CHEERING. ON THE THIRD
...E WON WITH 231-1/2 VOTES OUT OF 465.

...EVENING OF THE GREAT DAY, NOVEMBER
...OTHER CROWDS WERE CHEER-

NIGHT A NOISY CROWD OF FRIENDS LED BY A
SS BAND MARCHED TO THE LINCOLN HOME AN
LED FOR A SPEECH! ALL-NIGHT PARTIES
EBRATED LINCOLN'S NOMINATION.

THE MONTHS WHICH FOLLOWED HE GREW A B
AND HAD A STRANGE VISION OF HIMSELF AS
AS HE LAY GAZING ACROSS THE ROOM INTO

CHAPTER 8

PRESERVING THE UNION

Lincoln had been quiet during the four months between his election and inauguration, but everyone else had been loudly debating how to keep the country from splitting in half. Even before Election Day, South Carolina, Alabama, and Mississippi had warned that if Republicans won, they would hold constitutional conventions immediately thereafter. Most northerners, including Lincoln, did not take these threats seriously, given that the South had cried disunion many times before. Threatening secession was the southern states' way of intimidating northern politicians into conceding compromises friendly to the South. They had used the tactic so often over the previous two decades it had lost all credibility. Lincoln thought the South had "too much good sense" to ruin the government.

He was wrong. On December 20, 1860, South Carolina adopted an ordinance of secession. By February 1861, Florida, Mississippi, Alabama, Georgia, Louisiana, and Texas had joined. Jefferson Davis was named President of the new Confederate States of America a month before Lincoln was sworn in as president of the now dis-United States. Attempts at compromise to keep the Union together once again pandered to southern interests. Lincoln was against one such compromise, but tacitly endorsed another that would have led to a 13th amendment protective of slavery, the exact opposite of the actual 13th amendment passed four years later. None of the compromise bills succeeded.[1]

OPPOSITE: Lincoln, the presidential candidate

Inauguration and Cabinet

On the morning of March 4, Lincoln shared a carriage to the Capitol with outgoing President James Buchanan for the swearing-in ceremony. Other than mildly stating his opinion that secession was illegal, Buchanan had done nothing to stop it. His own cabinet had worked to aid and abet the South in the vacuum that his inaction had created. Prior to taking the oath, Lincoln offered a long address in which he attempted to soothe tensions, noting that the government had no intention of abolishing slavery in the South: "In your hands, my dissatisfied fellow countrymen, and not in mine, is the momentous issue of civil war." He ended with a somber plea:

> *I am loathe to close. We are not enemies, but friends. We must not be enemies. Though passion may have strained, it must not break our bonds of affection. The mystic chords of memory, stretching from every battle-field, and patriot grave, to every living heart and hearthstone, all over this broad land, will yet swell the chorus of the Union, when again touched, as surely they will be, by the better angels of our nature.*[2]

Lincoln was conciliatory but firm. Most in the North saw his inaugural address as a moderate hand reaching out to their brethren in the South. The South saw it as an act of war.

Meanwhile, Lincoln was putting the final touches on his new cabinet, which was truly a team of rivals. He chose as secretary of state none other than William Seward, the man he had unexpectedly bested for the nomination. Seward agreed reluctantly at first, but then saw himself as the power behind the throne, a prime minister of sorts to the man he still saw as inferior. Seward's attitude evolved over time, but in the beginning he was as much a competitor for power as he was a partner.

Lincoln's struggles with Seward were mild compared with those he had with Salmon P. Chase, the man he appointed secretary of the treasury. Chase would never come to terms with the railsplitter he felt was his infinite inferior (an opinion he no doubt applied to virtually everyone). Despite his backroom intrigues, Chase became a valuable cog who found ways to finance a long and expensive war. Filling out the cabinet were former rivals Simon Cameron (secretary of war, although he would be replaced

ABOVE: William Seward. OPPOSITE: Lincoln's first inauguration, March 4, 1861.

in less than a year by another rival, Edwin Stanton), Edward Bates (attorney general), Gideon Welles (secretary of the navy), Montgomery Blair (postmaster), and Caleb Smith (secretary of the interior).[3]

And the War Came

Barely a month after his inauguration, Lincoln had to decide what to do about Fort Sumter in the harbor of Charleston, South Carolina. The seceded state's newly formed rebel army had laid siege to the federal fort, demanding it be turned over.

After a great debate with his cabinet, Lincoln decided to provide much-needed food and clothing supplies—but no weapons—to the beleaguered island citadel. Before the materials could arrive, though, the secessionists began a bombardment on April 12, 1861. Commander Major Robert Anderson, who had mustered a young Lincoln into service in the Black Hawk War so many years before, was forced to surrender the fort. The Civil War had officially begun.

Lincoln immediately called for all northern states to provide 75,000 troops to protect the nation's capital and all federal facilities. Reaction from the upper states of the South was as quick as it was catastrophic. Lincoln's call for troops put these states, initially hesitant to join their colleagues in the Deep South, in a position to choose sides.

Virginia, North Carolina, Tennessee, and Arkansas quickly seceded and joined the Confederacy. Jefferson Davis moved his capital from Montgomery, Alabama, to Richmond, Virginia—ominously close to Washington. The southern-leaning Maryland also considered secession, but ultimately stayed in the Union. The Confederate States of America now comprised eleven states. Bordering states remaining with the Union but retaining slavery were Delaware, Maryland, Kentucky, and Missouri.[4]

ABOVE: The attack on Fort Sumter

The initial period of service for Union soldiers was three months, given that Lincoln (and nearly everyone else) assumed a quick resolution to a presumably minor conflict. The attack on Fort Sumter galvanized northerners, and the 75,000-men quota was filled almost instantaneously. However, trouble occurred from the beginning: secessionists in Baltimore, the same city where assassins had plotted to kill Lincoln as he passed through on his way to Washington, now did everything they could to thwart the passage of troops from Massachusetts and other points north to the nation's capital. They ripped up railroad tracks and burned bridges, and mobs attacked soldiers, resulting in the deaths of four soldiers and twelve civilians.

Lincoln pursued his initial actions without the input of Congress, which came back into session on July 1, 1861. In his first message to Congress, Lincoln noted that the United States government must "demonstrate to the world that those who can fairly carry an election can also suppress a rebellion; that ballots are the rightful and peaceful successors of bullets, and that when ballots have fairly and constitutionally decided there can be no successful appeal back to bullets." The election had fairly decided the results, and the South could not legally secede.

Battles and Generals

With little experience administering an executive branch of government, much less a wartime military, Lincoln called on aging war hero Winfield Scott to be general-in-chief. Meanwhile, Lincoln, ever the bookworm, sought to expand his own knowledge of military strategy, beginning with General Henry Halleck's *Elements of Military Art and Science*. He rapidly concluded that the Union's focus should be decimating the South's armies rather than taking territory.[5]

Within weeks, Lincoln and Scott had envisioned a blockade of all southern ports and points west, to be followed by an advance down the Mississippi River to cut the Confederacy in two. Opponents widely derided the plan as overly passive—they mockingly named it the "Anaconda" plan after the large constrictor snake. At the onset of the war the plan was also impractical, given the lack of Union naval vessels needed to enforce it. Ultimately, it would mirror the eventual means by which the North won the war.

ABOVE: Winfield Scott. FOLLOWING: Map of the "Anaconda" plan.

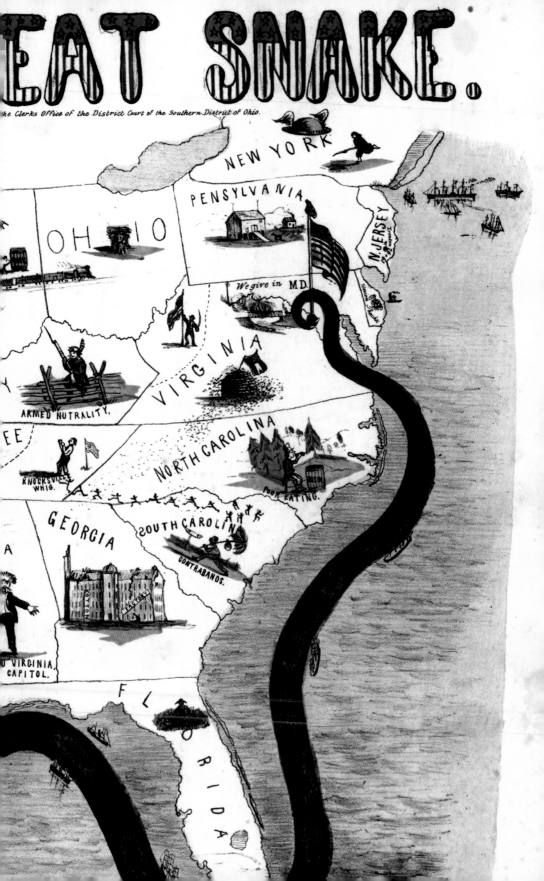

Before the plan could be implemented, the first battle caused shock waves in the capital. On July 21, 1861, the first Battle of Bull Run (sometimes called the Battle of Manassas) was fought between Union and Confederate forces merely 25 miles from Washington, D.C. Incredible though it seems today, hundreds of carriages carrying picnickers streamed out from the city to observe what both sides expected to be a quick and decisive end to a short-lived war. After initial gains by Union forces under General Irvin McDowell, Confederate forces led by General P.G.T. Beauregard and reinforced by General Joseph Johnston counterattacked, stimulating a panicked retreat of McDowell's forces back to Washington. Confederate General Thomas J. Jackson famously stood his ground, forever earning his sobriquet, Stonewall Jackson.[6]

With Union forces in disarray and proximity to the capital a grave concern, Lincoln was understandably apprehensive. But Confederate forces were also shocked by the brutality and casualties of battle and could not further attack the city. Both sides realized it would be a long and drawn-out war.

The embarrassing loss sent Winfield Scott to retirement and left Lincoln desperately searching for a military leader (most of the best had joined the Confederacy). With few options, he turned to a young George B. McClellan for his next general-in-chief. The Ohio-born McClellan had exhibited strong leadership in two small skirmishes in western Virginia, and he came highly recommended by Ohio Governor William Dennison and Ohio native Treasury Secretary Salmon P. Chase.

McClellan masterfully outfitted and drilled his raw recruits into a skilled Army of the Potomac, yet he consistently refused to put them into action. He repeatedly claimed the Confederates vastly outnumbered him, even though he had up to twice as many troops at his disposal. His soldiers loved him, but McClellan's overabundance of caution led to Lincoln's significant frustration. Adding insult, McClellan arrogantly considered himself vastly superior to the President, referring to Lincoln in letters home to his wife as "nothing more than a well-meaning baboon" and "a gorilla."[7]

TOP: Stonewall Jackson. MIDDLE: George McClellan. ABOVE: Salmon P. Chase.

Peninsula Campaign

McClellan rarely communicated his strategy or progress to his commander in chief. His insubordination included ignoring the president and retiring to bed after Lincoln had sat patiently in McClellan's parlor for an hour waiting for him to return from an evening out. Continuing to press his generals to fight, Lincoln suggested that the well-trained army make a frontal assault on Confederate forces between Washington and Richmond. McClellan disagreed, eventually proposing a complicated plan to take the Confederate capital of Richmond from the South, which was in direct opposition to Lincoln's strategy to defeat armies, not take territory.

After several months of obsessive planning, in March 1862 McClellan began shipping troops down the Potomac River to the Virginia peninsula between the James and York Rivers. The size of the troop movement was unprecedented, with more than 120,000 men, a dozen artillery batteries, and tons of equipment all ferried into place at the base of the peninsula. To Lincoln's chagrin, further overland movement toward Richmond was painfully slow because of bad weather, mud, and McClellan's exaggerated opinion of enemy troop strength. The Union forces negated the advantage of surprise, and by the time they advanced toward Richmond the more mobile Confederate army had positioned itself to defend the southern capital. Meanwhile, McClellan, against Lincoln's wishes, had left the Union capital woefully unprotected.[8]

ABOVE: The Penninsula Campaign, during the Siege of Yorktown.   FOLLOWING: *The Battle of Bull Run.*

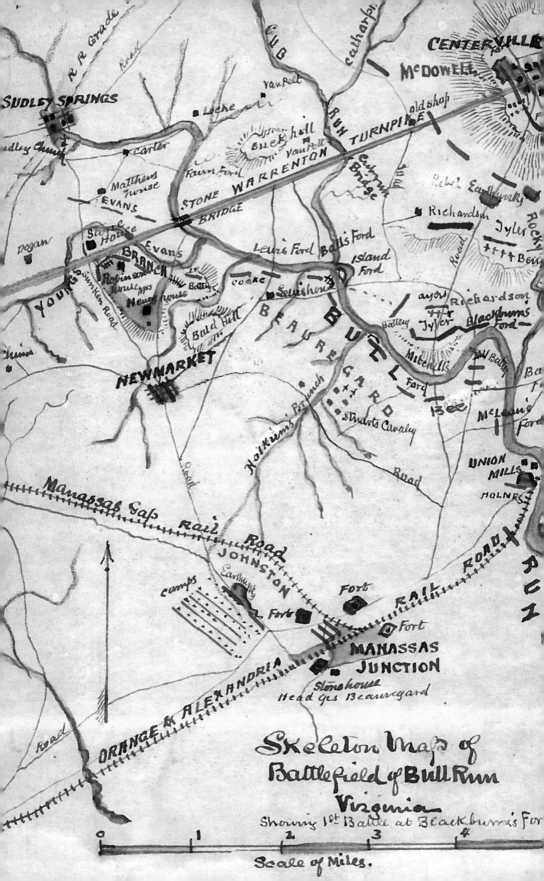

Skeleton Map of Battlefield of Bull Run Virginia Showing 1st Battle at Blackburn's Ford

By any measurement, the Peninsula Campaign was a disaster. The Union survived its critical blunder only because of Lincoln's strategic decision-making. McClellan, of course, blamed Lincoln for his supposed meddling. A frustrated Lincoln demoted McClellan. This left the president once again in desperate need of a military leader. Generals Henry Halleck, Ambrose Burnside (whose trademark facial hair was the inspiration for the term "sideburns"), Joseph Hooker, John C. Fremont, John McClernand, John Pope, George Meade, and others were all considered by Lincoln but ultimately found wanting. Sitting in the wings were Ulysses S. Grant and William T. Sherman, western generals who had not yet captured the president's eye.

McClellan's demotion was short-lived. In utter desperation and after several disastrous Union losses in the summer of 1862, Lincoln once again turned to McClellan as his General-in-Chief.

At the time, Lincoln was experiencing personal heartbreak in addition to the pressure of mounting Union soldier casualties. In February, Mary Lincoln had planned a grand open house to show off the dramatic and expensive improvements she had made to the aging and neglected White House. By the night of the party, however, Lincoln's two youngest sons had become severely ill. While guests gathered downstairs, Lincoln and Mary repeatedly slipped upstairs to check on their ailing children. Diagnosed with what was likely typhoid fever, Willie progressively worsened. On February 20, 1862, he died. Tad recovered, but never really understood the sudden loss of his older brother and constant playmate.

Mary was devastated, and for the rest of her time as First Lady (a term she coined to refer to her position) she wore nothing but black. Mary became an even greater burden on household staff and the growing list of Washington insiders who despised her. Lincoln mourned as well, coping by throwing himself more deeply into the continued struggle to save the Union. One part of that struggle was the hugely important battle of Antietam.

TOP: Mary Todd Lincoln in mourning black.   ABOVE: Willie Lincoln.
OPPOSITE: Map of the Battle of Bull Run
FOLLOWING: Company C, 41st New York Infantry, near Bull Run, August, 1862

Antietam

In September 1862, Confederate General Robert E. Lee led his Army of Northern Virginia into western Maryland. Following their victory at a second battle of Bull Run, Lee moved his army north to a point near Sharpsburg, alongside Antietam Creek, where they took up defensive positions. With surprising aggressiveness, McClellan's Army of the Potomac attacked Lee's forces on September 17. The first assault came from Union General Joseph Hooker on Lee's left flank, while General Ambrose Burnside later attacked the right. A surprise counterattack from Confederate General A.P. Hill helped push back Union forces. Eventually, Lee's troops withdrew from the battlefield first. He moved his remaining army back across the Potomac into the safety of Virginia.[8]

Always overly cautious, McClellan made no effort to follow. Lee had committed all of his 55,000 men, while McClellan only ordered a portion of his larger 87,000-man force into the fray. This numerical imbalance allowed Lee to create and exploit tactical advantages he should not have had. When questioned by Lincoln about his failure to pursue Lee, McClellan complained that his army and horses were sore-tongued and fatigued, and thus required rest. Lincoln responded tersely by telegram:

> *Will you pardon me for asking what the horses of your army have done since the battle of Antietam that fatigue anything?*[9]

ABOVE: Photograph from the Battle of Antietam, *Federal Buried, Rebel Unburied*
OPPOSITE: Map of the Battle of Antietam showing the movement of Lee's Confederate line
FOLLOWING: Union troops advance during the Battle of Antietam

Sept. 16 + 17th 1862

ROHRERSVILLE.

SPRINGVALE.

KEEDYSVILLE

BRIDGE No 1

KEEDYSVILLE ROAD

PORTERSTOWN

BURNSIDE 16th

BURNSIDE

ANTIETAM CREEK

PORTER

BATTERIES

SUMNER, 17th

MANSFIELD 17th

DUNKARDS

HOOKER, 17th

D.R. MILLERS HOUSE

BURNSIDE, 17th

HOOKER, 16th

MEADE

REBEL LINE, Sept. 18

NATIONAL CEMETERY

REBEL LINE, Sept. 16

HAGERSTOWN

SHARPSBURG

REBEL LINE, Sept. 17

REBEL LINE, Sept. 17

JACKSON

Left Frank

REBEL LINE, Sept. 17

Lee's Head Qurs 18th

Retreat of Lee's Army 18 Sept.

POTOMAC

CANAL

CANAL

POTOMAC

C. & O. CANAL

Ford

According to Swinton's History The union loss was 12.321 in
Killed. wounded. and missing. The Rebel loss was 5.309.
Longstreets (1st Corps) lost 3.415. Kr. w + missing Jacksons (2d Corps) 1.894 = 5309

Antietam was destined to be the single bloodiest day of battle in American history. The casualties for both armies totaled a staggering 22,717 dead, wounded, or missing.[10]

Despite Lincoln's frustration, Antietam stood out as an important battle in the fight for freedom. Although essentially a draw, the fact that Lee withdrew from the battlefield first allowed the North to record Antietam as a victory, something that Lincoln had been needing for some time.

Emancipation of the Slaves

The first emancipation of slaves, although short-lived, occurred in August 1861, when General John C. Fremont, the Republican nominee for president five years earlier and leader of Union forces in the West, issued a proclamation of martial law in Missouri. Fremont proclaimed that anyone under suspicion of being the enemy could be arrested and tried under military tribunals, and that slaves of rebels were to be seized and "declared freemen."

Lincoln was not happy. He had argued that emancipation could not be forced on any state in which slavery already existed, and Missouri had been admitted to the Union as a slave state. Under the War Powers Act, only the president could emancipate slaves, not generals in the field. Furthermore, the action hurt the war cause by endangering the delicate relations with border slave states Lincoln had worked so hard to keep in the Union. Lincoln placidly suggested that Fremont withdraw his order. When Fremont refused, Lincoln declared it void. As Lincoln expected, border slave states like Maryland, Kentucky, and Missouri emitted a deep sigh of relief and promptly provided more than 40,000 new troops to the war effort. In May 1862, Lincoln also rejected a similar proclamation in the field by General David Hunter.[11]

Lincoln was not oblivious to the idea of emancipation that early in his presidency. Mary had become deeply attached to Elizabeth Keckley, her dressmaker and confidante. Keckley had dressed other elite society ladies in Washington, including the wives of Jefferson Davis and Robert E. Lee prior to their

TOP: General John C. Fremont. ABOVE: Elizabeth Keckley.

departure for the Confederacy. Keckley and other free blacks working in the White House were constant reminders of the tentative nature of black citizenship (which the Dred Scott case had all but invalidated).[12] Meanwhile, radical Republicans in Congress were pressing Lincoln to emancipate the slaves as punishment for secession. Abolitionist leaders like William Lloyd Garrison and former slave Frederick Douglass were adamant that Lincoln simply abolish slavery with a stroke of a pen.

Lincoln viewed the issue as part of a more complicated picture. The war, as he saw it privately and explained publicly, was about preserving the Union, not abolishing slavery. He had to walk a fine line in his attempts to keep border states—all of which still had legal slavery—in the Union. The slightest misstep could send them into the hands of the Confederacy. Repeated attempts to encourage gradual, compensated emancipation, either with or without colonization of ex-slaves overseas, failed to get commitments from the border states. Keeping them in the Union was critical. To make this point clear, early in the war Lincoln said: "I hope to have God on my side, but I must have Kentucky."[13]

By the early spring of 1862, Lincoln had privately decided to issue an emancipation order. But he kept this decision to himself for many months while secretly drafting his arguments. Meanwhile, he publicly voiced apprehension about such a decision, suggesting that turning the rationale of the war from maintaining the Union to freeing the slaves would cause significant loss of northern support, in addition to creating potentially disastrous implications in the border states.[14]

In April 1862, at Lincoln's urging, Congress emancipated slaves in the District of Columbia and compensated their owners. That June, Lincoln signed a bill prohibiting slavery in all current and future U.S. territories. Most of these steps went largely unnoticed to anyone not directly affected, but they helped move public sentiment toward freedom. Unknown to anyone, Lincoln was preparing a draft of the now-famous document as he shuttled between the Soldier's Home where he spent his summers and the telegraph office of the War Department.

On July 13, 1862, Lincoln presented his preliminary draft to Secretary of State William Seward and Secretary of the Navy Gideon Welles. Both men were caught off guard, but after discussions and suggested changes to the text they agreed to what Lincoln was proposing. Seward warned, however, that the action might sound desperate, given the recent Union losses on the battlefield. He suggested Lincoln wait until after a Union victory. Lincoln agreed.

FOLLOWING: Lincoln's first draft of the Emancipation Proclamation

In pursuance of the sixth section of the act of congress entitled "An act to suppress insurrection and to punish treason and rebellion, to seize and confiscate property of rebels, and for other purposes" Approved July 17. 1862, and which act, and the Joint Resolution explanatory thereof, are herewith published, I, Abraham Lincoln, President of the United States, do hereby proclaim to, and warn all persons within the contemplation of said sixth section to cease participating in, aiding, countenancing, or abetting the existing rebellion, or any rebellion against the government of the United States, and to return to their proper allegiance to the United States, on pain of the forfeitures and seizures, as within and by said sixth section provided—

And I hereby make known that it is my purpose, upon the next meeting of congress, to again recommend the adoption of a practical measure for tendering pecuniary aid to the free choice or rejection, of any and all states, which may then be recognizing and practically sustaining the authority of the United States, and which may then have voluntarily adopted, or thereafter may voluntarily adopt, gradual abolishment ~~adoption~~ of slavery within such state or states— that the object is to practically restore, thenceforward to be maintain, the constitutional relation between the general government, and each, and all the states, wherein that relation is now suspended, or disturbed; and that, for this object, the war, as it has been, will be, prosecuted. And, as a fit and necessary military measure for effecting this object, I, as Commander-in-Chief of the Army and Navy of the United States, do order and declare that on the first day of January, in the year of our Lord one thousand, eight hundred and sixty three, all persons held as slaves within any state or states, wherein the constitutional authority of the United States shall not then be practically recognized, submitted to, and maintained, shall then, thenceforward, and forever, be free;

COME AND J[O]

PUBLISHED BY THE SUPERVISORY COMM[...]

1210 CHES[...]

⫻ US BROTHERS.

OR RECRUITING COLORED REGIMENTS
PHILADELPHIA.

Meanwhile, on August 19, New York *Tribune* editor and staunch abolitionist Horace Greeley, perhaps alerted that something was afoot, published an editorial he called "A Prayer for Twenty Millions," suggesting it was time for the administration to act on the slavery question. Three days later, Lincoln published a reply that somewhat surreptitiously explained his objective in the war:

> *I would save the Union. I would save it the shortest way under the Constitution. The sooner the national authority can be restored; the nearer the Union will be 'the Union as it was.' If there be those who would not save the Union unless they could at the same time save slavery, I do not agree with them. If there be those who would not save the Union unless they could at the same time destroy slavery, I do not agree with them. My paramount object in this struggle is to save the Union, and is not either to save or to destroy slavery. If I could save the Union without freeing any slave I would do it, and if I could save it by freeing all the slaves I would do it; and if I could save it by freeing some and leaving others alone I would also do that. What I do about slavery, and the colored race, I do because I believe it helps to save the Union; and what I forbear, I forbear because I do not believe it would help to save the Union. I shall do less whenever I shall believe what I am doing hurts the cause, and I shall do more whenever I shall believe doing more will help the cause. I shall try to correct errors when shown to be errors; and I shall adopt new views so fast as they shall appear to be true views.*[15]

As the world read this, no one knew Lincoln had already drafted his proclamation. His goal for months had been to influence public sentiment so citizens were prepared to accept what he was about to do. In September, the battle of Antietam was considered enough of a victory to heed Seward's caution, and on September 22, 1862, Lincoln issued the Emancipation Proclamation.

Written in dry, legal language, the proclamation stipulates that on:

> *…the first day of January [1863], all persons held as slaves within any state, or designated part of a state, the people shall then be in rebellion against the United States shall be then, thenceforward, and forever free…*[16]

PREVIOUS: Civil War recruitment broadside seeking to recruit African-American soldiers

The initial reaction was as Lincoln expected. Many of the more radical Republicans were ecstatic, while Democrats and other "peace at all costs" proponents saw it as an unnecessarily extreme act. Many voters agreed; Republicans lost twenty-eight seats in the House of Representatives that November. As Lincoln feared, many northerners were vehemently opposed to a civil war to free the slaves as opposed to preserve the Union.

Despite these setbacks, Lincoln was confident that the proclamation was both just and necessary. He explained that his action was solely as a war measure; that is, the proclamation was necessary to deprive the South of slave labor so important to their troop movements. With the danger of losing the border states in mind, the proclamation did not free any slaves in those states or any state or part of state now controlled by the Union. The only slaves who were freed were those in the Confederacy, where the federal government was powerless to enforce their freedom. Some have argued that this made the proclamation meaningless, but it did lead to the escape of many southern slaves into Union divisions. As Union forces captured more territory, freedom slowly spread to a broader group of southern-held slaves.

The Final Emancipation Proclamation was issued on January 1, 1863. In addition to declaring freedom for slaves in the designated areas, it was also a call for the enlistment of black soldiers. Many freemen as well as escaped slaves joined the Union military. Discrimination was still rampant in the North—black companies were segregated and required a white commanding officer—but for the first time blacks had an opportunity to defend their own liberty.

Despite the proclamation, the war continued into the spring and summer of 1863, culminating in a bloody and dramatic three-day battle that marked the turning point of the entire war and was eulogized in Lincoln's single most eloquent piece of spoken rhetoric.

THE 15TH OF APRIL, 1861, PRESIDENT LINCOLN
NT OUT A CALL FOR SEVENTY-FIVE THOUSAND
LUNTEERS TO PUT DOWN THE ARMED REBELLIO
THE SIX SOUTHERN STATES NAMED.

ON THE 17TH, VIRGINIA LEFT THE UNION----
AND THE NEXT DAY THE ARMS FACTORY AND

THE ANSWER FROM THE PEOPLE OF THE NORT
STATES WAS SWIFT AND ENTHUSIASTIC. URG
RELIGIOUS, SOCIAL AND POLITICAL LEADER
YOUNG MEN RUSHED TO ENLIST.

THE UNITED STATES NAVY YARD IN NORFO
ED LIKELY TO BE CAPTURED BY THE REBEL
... SO THE COMMANDING OFFICER ORDERED
... R MATERIAL BLOW

CHAPTER 9

FROM GETTYSBURG TO RE-ELECTION

L incoln hoped the spring thaw would bring a speedy end to the war, but he was to be disappointed. Union forces won several small skirmishes in Louisiana in April, a larger victory in May at Port Gibson, Mississippi, led by a general Lincoln had barely heard of, Ulysses S. Grant. The month of May also saw Union success at Fredericksburg, Virginia, and then some larger wins in Louisiana and Mississippi. But the spring also saw some Confederate victories, most notably the Battle of Chancellorsville.

Still looking for a reliable general, in January 1863 Lincoln put General Joseph Hooker in command of the Army of the Potomac, replacing General Ambrose Burnside. Hooker had been critical of both Burnside and Lincoln, so Lincoln wrote Hooker a letter to make sure he understood Lincoln was not entirely satisfied. Lincoln praised Hooker for his bravery and skill as a soldier, as well as his confidence. But he also warned Hooker that while his ambition was good "within reasonable bounds," he believed Hooker "had taken counsel of [his] ambition, and thwarted [General Burnside]'s command, which "did a great wrong to the country." He went on:

> I have heard…of your recently saying that both the Army and the Government needed a Dictator. Of course it was not for this, but in spite of it, that I have given you the command. Only those generals who gain successes, can set up dictators. What I now ask of you is military success, and I will risk the dictatorship.

OPPOSITE: An idealized portrait of Lincoln.   ABOVE: General Joseph Hooker.

Promising that the government would support him as much as it could, Lincoln warned Hooker he feared the negative spirit he created would infuse the Army and make his leadership difficult. Urging him to do his best, Lincoln ended with:

"And now, beware of rashness. Beware of rashness, but with energy, and sleepless vigilance, go forward, and give us victories." [1]

On April 30, Hooker threw his Army of the Potomac against Confederate General Robert E. Lee's Army of Northern Virginia just outside the village of Chancellorsville. Even though Hooker had more than twice as many troops as Lee, the series of battles continued until May 6. During the battle, Lee decided to split his army into two in order to strategically attack Hooker's main army while deflecting the advance of the right flank. Lincoln and others had encouraged splitting Hooker's army in similar fashion, but Hooker timidly retreated to a defensive position. Lee attacked Hooker's lines repeatedly with heavy casualties on both sides. It was a rout by the Confederates, although the hard battle and number of casualties kept Lee from wiping out the Union troops completely. [2]

Embarrassed by the horrific defeat, Hooker offered his resignation. No longer worried about a dictatorship, Lincoln immediately accepted and put General George Meade in charge of the Army of the Potomac.

Gettysburg and Vicksburg

The summer heat caused Washington's swamps to smell, and with it came the usual sicknesses caused by poor hygiene and even poorer sanitation. (Illness was a constant threat during the Civil War; Willie Lincoln had died because of impure water taken from the Potomac River, while soldiers were twice as likely to be killed by disease as by an enemy bullet). Escaping to his summer residence at the Soldier's Home three miles north of the White House, Lincoln pondered the next steps of the war.

He did not have to wait long. Emboldened by his victory at Chancellorsville, Robert E. Lee slowly moved his army through northwestern Virginia and up to Pennsylvania. Lee planned to circle Washington and put pressure on northern politicians to give up the fight. Lincoln pressed General Meade to pursue Lee and conquer his army once and for all. The two great armies, Meade with the Union Army of the Potomac and Lee with the Army of Northern Virginia, met at Gettysburg, Pennsylvania, in a turning point of the war.[3]

July 1, 1863, was the first of three days of brutal fighting. At first Union forces seemed to hold the best defensive positions, but soon the Confederate soldiers routed them. On the second day, Lee sent his armies' at the Union's flank, leading to brutal fighting at Little Round Top, the Devil's Den, and the Peach Orchard. Culp's Hill and the appropriately named Cemetery Hill became bloody battlefields. On the third day, after failing to breach Union lines on its left and right flanks, Lee ordered more than 12,000 men to attack the center of Meade's army on Cemetery Ridge, resulting in the disastrous and largely suicidal, Pickett's Charge.

The three-day battle caused between 46,000 and 51,000 total casualties, and ended with Lee retreating south.

Meade, who had been in command of the Army of the Potomac for only three days, managed a significant win at Gettysburg, but chose not to aggressively pursue Lee's escaping army, instead allowing their escape back across the Potomac. Lincoln was not pleased. He wrote an angry letter to Meade on July 14 noting that while he was very grateful for Meade's "magnificent success" on the battlefield, he was greatly distressed by the decision not to pursue and destroy Lee's army.

OPPOSITE: Battle of Chancelorsville. ABOVE: General George Meade. FOLLOWING: Battle of Gettysburg.

I do not believe you appreciate the magnitude of the misfortune involved in Lee's escape. He was within your easy grasp, and to have closed upon him would…have ended the war. As it is, the war will be prolonged indefinitely.…Your golden opportunity is gone, and I am distressed immeasurably because of it. [4]

Lincoln apparently had second thoughts about his censure of Meade and wrote on the envelope "To Gen. Meade, never sent, or signed." [5]

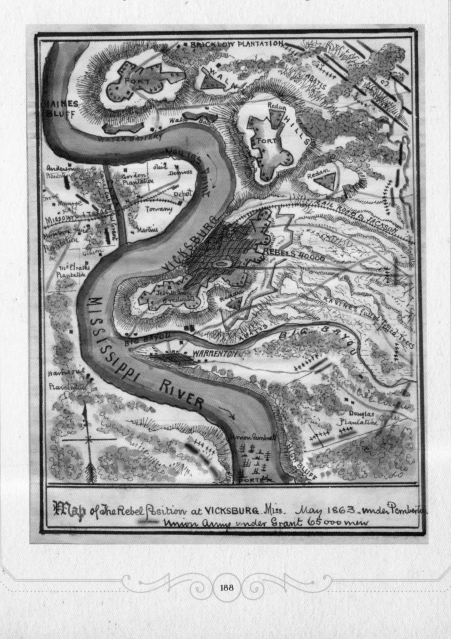

As the battle of Gettysburg was ending on July 3, so too was the long siege at Vicksburg. Ulysses S. Grant had started the war on the western front in Missouri and slowly worked his way toward the Mississippi River. Caught by surprise at the battle of Shiloh the previous year (Grant had been unprepared and slow to react), he was repeatedly chastised for the massive casualties accredited to his bare-knuckle fighting style and alleged drunkenness. When pressed for his removal, Lincoln refused, reportedly saying "I can't spare this man; he fights!" In mid-May, Grant's army took on the Confederate stronghold at Vicksburg.

OPPOSITE: Map of the Rebel position at Vicksburg
ABOVE: General Robert E. Lee.   FOLLOWING: Battle of Shiloh.

After diligently pressing the original Anaconda plan to blockade the coasts and cut the South in two by controlling the length of the Mississippi River, the last bastion was the fortress at Vicksburg. Several attempts to capture the city were unsuccessful, so on May 18 Grant settled in for a siege, cutting off supply lines. On July 4, the Confederates under General John Pemberton surrendered. The Union had cut the South in two, with the states west of the Mississippi River— Arkansas, Louisiana, Texas—now isolated from reinforcements.

Following Vicksburg, Lincoln promoted Grant to major general and gave him command of a newly formed Division of the Mississippi, where he directed several armies through major battles in the region. His skill and leadership would eventually lead Lincoln to commission him lieutenant general and command of all Union armies as general-in-chief, answering only to Lincoln.

PREVIOUS: Siege at Vicksburg.   ABOVE: Confederate dead at the edge of the Rose Woods, Gettysburg.

Gettysburg Address

Union victories were coming more frequently in the late summer and fall of 1863, although not universally, as a loss at Chickamauga and the New York draft riots would attest. But now it was time for a more somber occasion.

Because so many soldiers had perished at Gettysburg, a committee was set up to dedicate a cemetery to those who died there. Committee chairman David Wills invited the president to offer "a few appropriate remarks" to "formally set apart these grounds to their sacred use."

On a chilly November 19, Lincoln addressed the crowd after the oration by keynote speaker Edward Everett. Lincoln sat on the speaker's platform and listened to an opening prayer, music from the Marine Band, and Everett's two-hour discourse on "The Battles of Gettysburg." Following another short hymn sung by the Baltimore Glee Club, Lincoln rose to speak. He finished a mere two minutes later, so fleeting that many in the crowd largely missed his dedicatory remarks.

While Everett's much longer keynote, resplendent with neo-classical references and nineteenth-century rhetorical style, was well received, generations of elementary school students have memorized Lincoln's brief address. The irony of Lincoln observing "the world will little note nor long remember what we say here" is not lost on history.

Lincoln's remarks were designed both to dedicate the cemetery and redefine the objectives of the ongoing Civil War. The "four score and seven years ago" sets the beginning of the United States not at the Constitution, but the 1776 signing of the Declaration of Independence, where "all men are created equal." Those ideals were under attack, "testing whether that nation, or any nation so conceived and so dedicated, can long endure." After honoring the men who "struggled here," Lincoln reminds everyone still living what our role must be:

> It is rather for us to be here dedicated to the great task remaining before us—that from these honored dead we take increased devotion to that cause for which they gave the last full measure of devotion—that we here highly resolve that these dead shall not have died in vain—that this nation, under God, shall have a new birth of freedom—and that government of the people, by the people, for the people, shall not perish from the earth.[6]

FOLLOWING: Gettysburg Address

As he gave his address, Lincoln was already feeling the symptoms of variola, a mild form of smallpox, which kept him bedridden for weeks after his return to Washington. He eventually wrote out several copies of his address, including one sent to Everett to be joined with his own handwritten speech and sold at New York's Sanitary Commission Fair as a fundraiser for wounded soldiers.[7]

The War Continues

As much as Lincoln wanted the war to end, mixed battle results continued. Union victories in Tennessee, Florida, and Arkansas during the late fall of 1863 and into the winter were negated by Confederate successes in the South and the failure of the Red River campaign in the spring of 1864. Even victories by Union General Meade in Virginia were spoiled by Confederate General Lee's ability to escape each attack through strategic retreat. By this time Lincoln had promoted Grant to commander of all the Union armies and expressed his desire for Grant to "hold on with a bull-dog grip, and chew & choke, as much as possible."[8]

TOP: Photograph of Lincoln after Gettysburg Address
ABOVE: General Benjamin Butler.   OPPOSITE: General Unysses S. Grant.   FOLLOWING: Battle of Cold Harbor.

Lincoln liked Grant because the general was an aggressive fighter. But unlike the overly cautious McClellan, Grant's persistence increased casualty rates. As part of his Overland Campaign in early June 1864, Grant relentlessly attacked Lee's fortified defensive positions in the Battle of Cold Harbor. The number of killed or wounded Union soldiers in this fruitless battle was so tremendous that it led a Confederate officer to opine, "this is murder, not war." Both sides lost tens of thousands of lives during the Overland Campaign. When Lincoln asked Grant about his plans, he replied, "I propose to fight it out on this line if it takes all summer."[9]

In June, Grant attempted to capture the city of Petersburg, Virginia. General Benjamin Butler made the first assault but failed to break through the multiple lines of Confederate fortifications. Similar attempts by General Meade also failed, as did attempts to cut the railroad supply lines. For the next nine months, Grant and his generals repeatedly assaulted the city, building more than thirty miles of entrenchments to cut off supplies.

By July, Grant was looking for a way to shorten the siege, and Lieutenant Colonel Henry Pleasants offered up an idea. Pleasants had been a mining engineer before the war, and he proposed digging a horizontal mine shaft to a point underneath Confederate lines and planting explosive charges. The shaft was built, and on July 30 was set to go. While well planned, last-minute replacement of a well-trained and rested division of United States Colored Troops with exhausted white troops led to poor assault execution. A successful explosion (hence "The Crater" battle name) was followed by a disastrously inept frontal attack that failed miserably and caused nearly 4,000 needless casualties. The siege of Petersburg continued.[10]

While Grant was pressing Lee, Union General William Tecumseh Sherman was invading Georgia from the Union-controlled area around Chattanooga, Tennessee. Sherman slowly pushed toward Atlanta as the Confederate Army of Tennessee's General Joseph Johnston played a cautionary defensive game. But in July, Jefferson Davis replaced the despised Johnston with John Bell Hood, a hugely aggressive general who pushed back hard and created a standoff with Sherman that lasted for months.

TOP: Colonel Henry Pleasants. MIDDLE: General Philip Sheridan. ABOVE: General Jubal Early.

Lincoln was becoming increasingly desperate to finish the war. He authorized Grant to engage in destructive warfare, targeting and destroying plantations, railroads, bridges, crops, and anything that the Confederacy needed to sustain its troops. In the latter part of 1864, General Philip Sheridan burned fields and plantations in Virginia's Shenandoah Valley, while Sherman did the same in his March to the Sea through Georgia. Union forces left no possibility that Confederate forces could resupply soldiers along the way.

Meanwhile, Lincoln was literally coming under fire. Robert E. Lee sent Confederate General Jubal Early racing up the Shenandoah Valley to invade Maryland, disrupt Union rail-supply lines, and threaten Washington. Lee hoped this would force Grant to move troops away from him and Richmond in order to defend the capital. Success would also disrupt the November presidential election, and a Lincoln loss would change the trajectory of the war.

Lincoln was at the Soldier's Home when news of fighting at nearby Fort Stevens reached him. Against the wishes of his aides, Lincoln rode out to the fort to witness the assault firsthand. The Confederate threat was repulsed, but not before the exposed Lincoln was pulled down from his viewing point after a soldier next to him was killed by incoming fire. Some reports suggest it was future Supreme Court Justice Oliver Wendell Holmes who shouted at Lincoln, "Get down, you damn fool, before you get shot!"[11]

Election of 1864

The horrific casualties of the Overland Campaign, the stalemates at Petersburg and Atlanta, and a series of Confederate victories put Lincoln on edge during the summer and early fall of 1864. He believed he would lose the upcoming presidential election in November. Some in the North pressed for suspension of the election because of the ongoing war, but Lincoln insisted the democratic process was what they were fighting for, and that the election would continue as planned.

But public support for the war was growing frail. Inability to bring the war to a successful completion had people looking for ways to get out of it. Many in the North had gotten behind the idea of saving the Union but were not so enthusiastic about continuing to sacrifice their sons to free slaves. Copperheads in the North (named for the Liberty head they cut from large one-cent coins and wore

FOLLOWING: General Sherman's "March to the Sea"

as badges) wanted peace at any cost. Also known as "Peace Democrats," they distinguished themselves from "War Democrats" by seeking immediate conciliation with the South and a return to slavery.

To make matters worse, Lincoln's own treasury secretary, Salmon P. Chase, had been working behind his back for months to convince the Republican Party to eject Lincoln and nominate Chase in his stead. When Chase's scheme was uncovered, he offered his resignation. Lincoln, who had refused Chase's earlier resignation offers, accepted this one, writing, "And yet you and I have reached a point of mutual embarrassment in our official relation which it seems cannot be overcome."[12]

Lincoln was so convinced he would lose reelection that on August 23, 1864, he wrote what has become known as the "Blind Memorandum":

> *This morning, as for some days past, it seems exceedingly probable that this Administration will not be re-elected. Then it will be my duty to so co-operate with the President elect, as to save the Union between the election and the inauguration; as he will have secured his election on such ground that he cannot possibly save it afterward.*[13]

ABOVE: Battle of the Wilderness, part of the bloody Overland Campaign

He folded the memorandum in half, asked each member of his perplexed cabinet to sign the back without reading it, then put it away for safekeeping.

Lincoln's pessimism was justified, as the Democratic Party had selected Lincoln's former General-in-Chief, George B. McClellan, as their nominee. While arrogantly ineffectual as a fighter, McClellan was beloved by his troops for the care he took to train and outfit them. Lincoln was afraid that too many of the troops, tired of war and eager to return home to the families, would leave the Republican Party to vote for their former commanding officer.

Republicans were so concerned they formed a coalition with some War Democrats and renamed themselves the National Union Party, which set as a primary platform position the continued pursuit of the war until unconditional Confederacy surrender. The platform also included a constitutional amendment for the abolition of slavery. In an effort to facilitate anticipated reassimilation of southern civilians into the Union, former senator and current military governor of Tennessee—and staunch Unionist—Andrew Johnson was chosen to be Lincoln's vice presidential running mate (a decision that would have significant postwar ramifications).

But the Democratic Party fragmented again. In 1860 it split between Northern and Southern Democrats, and now in 1864 it split between Peace and War Democrats. Some of the latter had joined with Republicans, but most remained in the Democratic Party. Peace Democrats drove the party platform, which proposed a negotiated peace with the South, the very scenario Lincoln warned of in his still-secret "blind memorandum." Copperheads went even further, declaring the war a failure and demanding an immediate peace. Their own nominee, McClellan, rejected the peace platform, so the Democrats forced him to take on an avowed Copperhead, George Pendleton, as his vice presidential running mate.

In early September, Lincoln finally caught a break. Admiral David Farragut won the Battle of Mobile Bay, a quixotic Union campaign to capture the last harbor controlled by Confederates in the Gulf of Mexico. The harbor was protected by

ABOVE: Lincoln's handwritten Blind Memorandum
FOLLOWING: *The Peacemakers*, depicting the Union command's strategy session on the steamer *River Queen* during the final days of the Civil War

three onshore forts, three traditional wooden gunboats, and an imposing ironclad commanded by Roger Jones, the same man who had so impressively commanded the CSS *Virginia* against the USS *Monitor* in a battle of ironclads two years earlier. Mines (then called torpedoes) blocked the harbor entrance. Farragut became famous by being lashed to the rigging of the main mast and, according to legend, yelling, "Damn the torpedoes, full speed ahead."

Soon afterward, Sherman finally drew Confederate General John Bell Hood away from Atlanta, which allowed the Union to capture the Georgia capital. As northern newspapers praised the mighty successes at both Atlanta and Mobile Bay, Lincoln's reelection chances suddenly looked more promising.[14]

Indeed, by the time November arrived the election was not even close. The National Union Party received 55 percent of the popular vote (with only northern states voting, of course) to 45 percent for the Democratic Party. But the electoral vote was even more decisive: 212 for Lincoln and 21 for McClellan. Lincoln won 22 of the 25 northern states and was reelected in a landslide.

Next Steps

Immediately after the election Lincoln called a meeting of his cabinet and read them the blind memorandum in which he described his impending reelection loss. Everyone present had a hardy, but relieved, chuckle.

The humor, however, was short-lived—and the war continued. While the fall of Atlanta in early September had been instrumental in determining the election

ABOVE: Major General Sherman and staff in the trenches outside Atlanta

outcome, Sherman seemed to have fallen off the map. Only later did an anxious Lincoln learn what Sherman's army had been doing during the long autumn. Christmas arrived with the following dispatch from the southern front:

> *I beg to present you as a Christmas gift the city of Savannah with 150 heavy guns & plenty of ammunition & also about 25000 bales of cotton.*

Lincoln was ecstatic. Sherman had followed his capture of Atlanta by marching his men at an unprecedented speed through Georgia on a destructive path to the sea. The final conquest, coastal Savannah, cut the South in two, a severance from which they could not recover. Sherman then turned north to squeeze Confederate General Robert E. Lee's Army of Northern Virginia between himself and Union Army General Ulysses S. Grant's Army of the Potomac.

The day after Christmas, Lincoln wrote a long letter back to his itinerant general. He offered "many, many, thanks for your Christmas gift," and acknowledged his own doubts.

> *When you were about leaving Atlanta for the Atlantic coast, I was anxious, if not fearful; but feeling that you were the better judge, and remembering that 'nothing risked, nothing gained' I did not interfere. Now, the undertaking being a success, the honor is all yours; for I believe none of us went farther than to acquiesce....But what next? I suppose it will be safer if I leave Gen. Grant and yourself to decide.*[15]

The South never recovered. Instead of losing the election on terms that would have ensured the return of slavery and the permanent dismemberment of the Union, Lincoln was reelected and empowered to see the country begin its path to eventual reunification. Sherman's march to the sea was brutal, a "scorched earth" total war strategy that left devastation in its wake, but there is a strong argument for its ultimate effectiveness.[16]

As the nation's capital settled in to a frosty winter, Lincoln was looking forward to a successful and happy new year in 1865.

...ND AND BLOODIER BATTLE OF BULL RUN
...AGAINST THE UNION FORCES... ELEVEN
...AND UNION SOLDIERS WERE CAPTURED AT
...R'S FERRY... THEN IN SEPTEMBER ———

. CAME ANTIETAM! QUIET LITTLE ANTIETA...
...LOWED PAST A WHITE COUNTRY CHURCH, A...
...ELD AND A PASTURE. BEFORE THE BATTLE...
...CENE COULD HAVE BEEN MORE PEACEFUL...

...AND BOYS IN GRAY WERE KILLING EACH OTH...
...LOST TWELVE THOUSAND!

CHAPTER 10

OF MARTYRDOM AND LEGACY

The early part of 1865 seemed to put the Union on a path toward victory. By this time the Confederate armies were decimated, while the already larger Union armies were augmented by the United States Colored Troops, which comprised ex-slaves and freemen. Sherman's March to the Sea had reached Savannah before Christmas, and he was moving his army up through the Carolinas to rendezvous with Grant. Grant had been pressing the Siege of Petersburg for nearly nine months, and he continued to reduce the numbers and effectiveness of Lee's army. On April 1 and 2, Grant attacked the Army of Northern Virginia relentlessly, breaching the Confederate defenses and cutting off their supply lines. The siege was over and Lee was on the run, desperately trying to move west, then south, to meet up with other southern forces.

He never made it. Unlike the "slows" of former Army of the Potomac Generals McClellan and Meade, Grant aggressively followed Lee's Army of Northern Virginia, skirmishing at his rear and forcing him further west. Lee got as far as Appomattox Court House, where Grant's army surrounded him, thus forcing Lee's surrender on April 9.

Far from tranquility, the war's potential end brought instead a new set of problems for Lincoln. Always thinking ahead, he believed the Emancipation Proclamation was on weak grounds. Worried that after the end of hostilities his war measure would likely not have had the force of law, Lincoln had immediately pressed for a constitutional amendment to end slavery permanently. The Senate had passed it a year before, in April 1864, but the House was dragging its feet. They were finally getting ready to put it to a vote at the end of January 1865 after much cajoling, coercing, and perhaps compensation from Lincoln's administration. It would be a close vote.

OPPOSITE: Lincoln and Salmon P. Chase working on legislation
FOLLOWING: Lee surrenders to Grant, Appomattox Court House, April 9, 1865

M.D.Guillaume

Then a rumor spread that there were "peace commissioners" in Washington. Looking for a way to end the war without having to pass a constitutional amendment, many representatives wavered. They sent a message to the president asking if any such commissioners were in town. Lincoln employed a bit of deception, replying that there were no commissioners in the city of Washington and he did not expect any. The vote squeaked through.[1]

Of course, there were peace commissioners, but Lincoln had arranged for them to wait in Hampton Roads, Virginia, for a conference on board the steamboat *River Queen*. Lincoln had given a factually accurate, if incomplete, response to Congress. When Lincoln went to Hampton Roads a few days later he made it clear that any peace must include both reunification and an end to slavery. As expected, the southern commissioners, which included Confederate Vice President Alexander Stephens, did not agree to those conditions and went home to Richmond.[2]

Lincoln at City Point and Richmond

Hearing from Washington that Lincoln looked even more worn out than usual, in March General Grant invited Lincoln to City Point (near Petersburg). Lincoln immediately accepted. He was not alone; Mary insisted on joining him, so a party including Tad Lincoln, a maid, a bodyguard, and a military aide boarded the *River Queen* on March 23 for the trip. Son Robert, now an adjunct to Grant's army, met them on their arrival the next evening. Lincoln took time to visit the troops and confer with Generals Grant and Sherman and Admiral David Porter.

Overall it was a restful but productive visit. That changed when Mary Lincoln flew into a jealous rage at seeing General Ord's wife riding "too close" to her husband, after which Lincoln sent Mary back to Washington. Soon after her departure, however, the Union captured Richmond, which the Confederate leadership had abandoned. She insisted on returning, this time bringing a large entourage.

During Mary's absence, Lincoln took Tad into Richmond. After landing at the docks, Lincoln and Tad walked the mile or so to the Confederate White House that had served until a few days earlier as Jefferson Davis's office. Surrounding him along the way were hundreds of ex-slaves who wanted to see the "Great Emancipator," while anxious white southerners stared suspiciously from their windows.

OPPOSITE: Lincoln visiting the battlefield.   FOLLOWING: Lincoln at City Point.

On April 8, Lincoln visited the Depot Field Hospital at City Point. Over the course of a full day he shook the hands of more than 6,000 patients, including a few sick and wounded Confederate soldiers. Feeling the pressure of business, Lincoln left City Point to return to Washington on the evening of April 8. The next day, Lee surrendered his army to General Ulysses S. Grant, effectively ending the war.[3]

Jubilation and Heartbreak

The mood in Washington was euphoric. After four long years the war was nearly over. Lincoln had anticipated this ending in his second inaugural address, reminding northerners that they should welcome southerners back into the Union:

> With malice toward none, with charity for all, with firmness in
> the right as God gives us to see the right, let us strive on to finish
> the work we are in, to bind up the nation's wounds, to care for him
> who shall have borne the battle and for his widow and his orphan,
> to do all which may achieve and cherish a just and lasting peace
> among ourselves and with all nations.[4]

Not everyone agreed with Lincoln's "without malice" sentiment. Radical Republicans wanted the South to pay dearly for its treasonous actions. But those decisions would come later; now was the time for celebration. Buildings were decorated with patriotic red, white, and blue bunting; flags were everywhere and everyone seemed happy in the nation's capital.

Then tragedy. President and Mary Lincoln were joined at Ford's Theatre on Good Friday, April 14, by Major Henry Rathbone and his fiancée, Clara Harris. A night out to see the long-running comedy *Our American Cousin* would give Lincoln a chance to put thoughts of war behind him.[5]

During the performance, at about 10:14 p.m., actor and southern sympathizer John Wilkes Booth stealthily entered the rear of the box. He pressed a small derringer pistol to the back of Lincoln's head, and fired. After slashing with a dagger at Rathbone's arm, Booth climbed over the rail of the second-story theater box. He jumped, his spur catching on the American flag decorating the box. Booth hit the stage, breaking his leg. He shouted the Virginia state motto, "*sic semper tyrannis!*" ("thus ever to tyrants!") and raced out the back door and onto a

OPPOSITE: John Wilkes Booth. FOLLOWING: Assasination of President Lincoln.

waiting horse. It took an army of pursuers twelve days to catch up with Booth, who was finally shot and killed while hiding in a tobacco barn.

The unresponsive Lincoln was carried across the street to Petersen's boarding house, where he clung to life until the next morning, dying without regaining consciousness at 7:22. Secretary of War Edwin Stanton captured the moment with, "Now he belongs to the ages." The sixteenth president of the United States was dead just days after the long war that dominated his entire presidency had ended.

Lincoln's body lay in state in the White House before being loaded on a train for the long, arduous trip back to Springfield. The route retraced that which Lincoln had taken when he first came to Washington four years before, making many stops so that people could see him one last time. Millions more saw his train as it made its way home for burial in the Lincoln tomb at Oak Ridge Cemetery.[6]

Legacy

Almost immediately following his assassination, the process of elevating Lincoln to martyrdom began. That he was shot on Good Friday and died the next day invited parallels to Jesus Christ. While not everyone mourned his loss, many who vehemently disagreed with him during the war re-evaluated his contributions. Even many in the South felt bereaved: with Lincoln gone so too was the man

ABOVE: Booth jumping onto the stage after shooting Lincoln. OPPOSITE: Wanted poster for John Wilkes Booth and co-conspirators John E. Surratt, and David Herold. FOLLOWING: Alonzo Chappel's *The Last Hours of Abraham Lincoln*

War Department, Washington, April 20, 1865,

☞ $100,000 REWARD!

THE MURDERER

f our late beloved President, Abraham Lincoln,

IS STILL AT LARGE.

$50,000 REWARD

Will be paid by this Department for his apprehension, in addition to any reward offered by nicipal Authorities or State Executives.

$25,000 REWARD

Will be paid for the apprehension of JOHN H. SURRATT, one of Booth's Accomplices.

$25,000 REWARD

Will be paid for the apprehension of David C. Harold, another of Booth's accomplices.

LIBERAL REWARDS will be paid for any information that shall conduce to the arrest of either of the above-ed criminals, or their accomplices.

All persons harboring or secreting the said persons, or either of them, or aiding or assisting their concealment or pe, will be treated as accomplices in the murder of the President and the attempted assassination of the Secretary of e, and shall be subject to trial before a Military Commission and the punishment of DEATH.

Let the stain of innocent blood be removed from the land by the arrest and punishment of the murderers.

All good citizens are exhorted to aid public justice on this occasion. Every man should consider his own conscience ged with this solemn duty, and rest neither night nor day until it be accomplished.

EDWIN M. STANTON, Secretary of War.

DESCRIPTIONS.—BOOTH is Five Feet 7 or 8 inches high, slender build, high forehead, black hair, black eyes, and rs a heavy black moustache.

OHN H. SURRAT is about 5 feet, 9 inches. Hair rather thin and dark; eyes rather light; no beard. Would gh 145 or 150 pounds. Complexion rather pale and clear, with color in his cheeks. Wore light clothes of fine lity. Shoulders square; cheek bones rather prominent; chin narrow; ears projecting at the top; forehead rather and square, but broad. Parts his hair on the right side; neck rather long. His lips are firmly set. A slim man.

DAVID C. HAROLD is five feet six inches high, hair dark, eyes dark, eyebrows rather heavy, full face, nose short, d short and fleshy, feet small, instep high, round bodied, naturally quick and active, slightly closes his eyes when ing at a person.

NOTICE.—In addition to the above, State and other authorities have offered rewards amounting to almost one hun-thousand dollars, making an aggregate of about TWO HUNDRED THOUSAND DOLLARS.

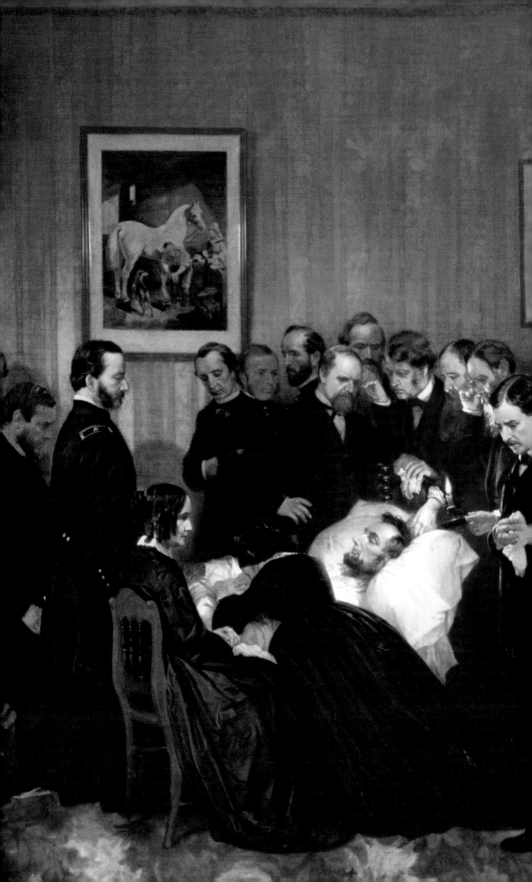

who stood in the way of the more aggressive elements in the North intent on punishing the South.

Within weeks, books were being written extolling his life. Some of these biographies reflected the inherent biases of the writers more than they did Lincoln's actual beliefs (for example, making him highly religious when he was not). Angered by false representations, Robert Lincoln authorized Lincoln's private secretaries, John Nicolay and John Hay, to pen the definitive biography. William Herndon, Lincoln's longtime law partner in Springfield, interviewed all the people who knew Lincoln he could find, and then struggled for years to write about Lincoln's early life. His three-volume biography was finally finished in 1889, after young journalist Jesse Weik provided assistance. Uncounted others have written about the man, over time creating, then breaking down, then creating new myths and legends as the public struggled to understand a man much more complicated than a simple rail-splitter candidate.

Today, Lincoln almost universally ranks at the top of any "best president of all time" poll, with both Democrats and Republicans claiming the mantle of Lincoln. Ironically, in the current era, the Democratic Party has a stronger case for this claim.

In the mid-nineteenth century, Republicans stood for inclusiveness, personal freedom, and positive government action. As a proud Republican, Lincoln championed federally funded internal improvements to build infrastructure, at one point arguing, "The legitimate object of government, is to do for a community of

people, whatever they need to have done, but cannot do, at all, or cannot, so well do, for themselves."[7] Today's Democratic Party reflects these characteristics more than the Republican Party does. This is due in large part to white Southerners abandoning the Democratic Party starting in the 1960s due to the party's support of civil rights. The Republican Party of the early twenty-first century bears more relationship to the anti-immigrant nativist Know-Nothing Party of the 1850s than the pro-Union, anti-slavery party of Lincoln.

Another aspect of Lincoln's legacy is the way he redefined the values of republicanism. While honoring the Constitution, Lincoln refocused attention on the basic objectives of the country as defined in the Declaration of Independence: freedom and equality for all. The "all" had been limited to white men, but Lincoln's actions began a cascade of civil rights actions that extended well beyond the Emancipation Proclamation.

In January of his last year, Lincoln pressed hard for passage of what would become the 13th amendment to the Constitution. This amendment abolished slavery and involuntary servitude, thus codifying the proclamation's goal that all slaves "shall be then, thenceforward, and forever free."[8] This was followed in 1868 by the 14th amendment, which granted U.S. citizenship to former slaves and instructed states to protect all citizens' rights and privileges and guarantee all persons equal protection under the law. This effectively overturned the Dred Scott decision. The 15th amendment in 1870 prohibited the use of race, color, or previous condition of servitude (aka slavery) in determining which citizens could vote.

OPPOSITE: Thomas Nast's celebration of Emancipation.   ABOVE: Abraham Lincoln's funeral.

In a little-known position taken early in his political career, Lincoln had suggested that the right to vote might be extended to women. Passage of the 19th amendment in 1920 finally accomplished this goal, prohibiting the government from denying women the right to vote on the same terms as men. Even the basic tenets of the Electoral College were influenced by Lincoln's decisions, as citizenship and right to vote for former slaves reduced the "slave benefit" of the South, which could no longer count three-fifths of the nonvoting slave population in determining the number of representatives each state was allowed.

Even the nation's great memorial to Abraham Lincoln in Washington, D.C., has continued to play a symbolic role in the progression of equal rights. Despite the equal rights amendments of the mid-1800s, pervasive discrimination and "black laws" that restricted the rights of African-American citizens were widespread throughout the country until well after World War II.

Although the opera singer Marian Anderson was world renowned for her exquisite contralto voice, in 1939 she was denied the right to sing for an integrated audience in Constitution Hall. First Lady Eleanor Roosevelt stepped in and arranged for Anderson to sing to a crowd of more than 75,000 (plus a radio audience) from the steps of the Lincoln Memorial. In 1963, on the 100th anniversary of the Emancipation Proclamation, the Lincoln Memorial was again the site of history when Martin Luther King Jr. stood on those same steps to deliver his famed "I Have a Dream" speech. King went on to spearhead passage of the 1965 Civil Rights Act and 1966 Voting Rights Act, both attempts to finally and fully secure the rights first codified in Lincoln's era.

Like Lincoln, King was martyred for his efforts.

Enduring Actions

As President, Abraham Lincoln was by necessity focused on the slavery question and the unbearable strife of Civil War. But other responsibilities did not stop during the war. In some ways it became easier to push the progressive programs Lincoln wanted because the South—usually the roadblock to such actions—was no longer represented in Congress. With Republicans in control of all three houses of power (House, Senate, White House), Lincoln and his allies were able to pass several substantial and legacy-bearing acts of law.

Some of these acts had been floating around Congress for many years, but representatives of southern states continued to block them. In 1862 the first of a series of Homestead Acts was finally passed, and Lincoln immediately signed it into law. The Act encouraged settlers to move west by offering up to 160 acres of public land, available for a small filing fee and the requirement to complete five years of continuous residence, after which the land became their permanent property. By giving away more than 80 million acres, the government effectively colonized most of the continent out to the west coast.

Also in 1862, Lincoln created a Department of Agriculture to bring science to farming. That same year Lincoln signed into law the Morrill Land-Grant Act, which provided federal lands for the creation of land-grant colleges across the United States. To maintain their status, colleges had to include programs in agriculture and engineering, as well as a Reserve Officers' Training Corps program.

Lincoln opened up the west in another way, by signing a pair of laws named the Pacific Railway Acts. These laws promoted the building of a transcontinental railroad between the eastern side of the Missouri River at Council Bluffs, Iowa, and the navigable waters of the Sacramento River. Jefferson Davis had been originally authorized to survey options (not surprisingly, he preferred a southern route). The second Act set the width of the tracks at exactly four feet and eight and one-half inches, which came to be known as the standard gauge and made it easier for different railroad companies to transfer cars.

In one of his least popular legacies, Abraham Lincoln also signed into law the first federal income tax, which provided much-needed funding for the war effort (in all fairness, the Confederacy also started an income tax).

In contrast, one of Lincoln's most beloved legacies was to formally establish the Thanksgiving holiday in November. Such a day of thanks had occurred sporadically before him and usually at the state level, but in 1863 he created the precedent for an annual day of Thanksgiving at the federal level.

Lincoln also set aside the first protected park on federally owned land. The Yosemite Grant of 1864 provided federal protection for the Yosemite Valley and Mariposa Grove in California. The land was then ceded over to the state to become the first California State Park. The park set the precedent for the National Park system. In 1890, at the urging of John Muir and Robert Underwood Johnson, Yosemite was returned to federal control as Yosemite National Park, now one of scores of National Parks around the United States.[9]

Lincoln left another environmental legacy. In 1863 he signed into creation the National Academy of Sciences. More than 150 years later, the National Academy has more than 2,300 members and remains true to its founding goals of "providing independent, objective advice to the nation on matters related to science and technology."

Keeping the Name Alive

In addition to the many schools, statues, memorials, and even aircraft carriers named after Abraham Lincoln, there are several organizations that work to keep Lincoln's name alive. These generally focus on honoring Lincoln's legacy and providing a forum for further study. Below are some of those organizations. Links to their websites can be found on page 247.

The **Abraham Lincoln Association** is based in Lincoln's adopted hometown of Springfield, Illinois. Organized in 1908, the association's purpose is to observe each anniversary of the birth of Abraham Lincoln, to preserve and make more accessible the landmarks associated with his life, and to actively encourage, promote, and aid the collection and dissemination of authentic information regarding all phases of his life and career. It publishes the *Journal of the Abraham Lincoln Association*, which remains the only journal devoted exclusively to the study of Abraham Lincoln. The association hosts an annual symposium and banquet on Lincoln's birthday and has a quarterly newsletter.

Similarly, **The Lincoln Forum** has a twenty-year history of bringing together people who share a deep interest in the life and times of Abraham Lincoln and the Civil War era. Founded by two preeminent Lincoln scholars, Frank J. Williams and Harold Holzer, the Forum holds an annual three-day conference in Gettysburg, Pennsylvania, culminating with the reenactment of Lincoln's Gettysburg Address on November 19. The forum also sponsors tours, student essay competitions, teacher scholarships, a biannual newsletter, and annual awards to recognize special contributions to the field of Lincoln studies. The ultimate goals of the Forum are to enhance the understanding and to preserve the memory of Abraham Lincoln.

Another organization, the **Abraham Lincoln Institute** based in Washington, D.C., provides free, ongoing education on the life, career, and legacy of Abraham Lincoln. The Institute's primary goal is to offer resources for educators, government and community leaders, and the general public. It holds an annual conference free to everyone, and offers additional symposia, seminars, lectures, and special events.

Also based in Washington, D.C., is the **Lincoln Group of the District of Columbia**. Organized in 1935, it is one of the nation's most active groups promoting the life of our sixteenth president. The Lincoln Group of D.C. holds monthly dinner lectures featuring prominent authors, a monthly book discussion group, annual symposia, and tours to the many Lincoln and Civil War sites in the District, Maryland, and Virginia area. The group publishes a quarterly newsletter, lays a wreath at the Lincoln Memorial on February 12 each year, and sponsors many outreach activities in the region. Because of its proximity to Congress and the White House, C-SPAN often covers these events for broadcast.

There are many other Lincoln groups in the United States. The **Lincoln Group of New York** holds three dinner meetings each year. Educational in nature, the group strives to promote fellowship and scholarship to all that are interested. Similarly, the **Lincoln Group of Boston** meets several times a year for informal lunches to allow members to discuss research and scholarship in the Lincoln field. The **Lincoln Association of Jersey City** (New Jersey), organized in 1865, is the longest active organization dedicated to Lincoln's memory. It holds an annual commemorative ceremony at a Lincoln Statue in Lincoln Park, Jersey City, followed by an annual dinner featuring Lincoln scholars. Other organizations include the **Lincoln Fellowship of Pennsylvania**, the **Lincoln Society in Peekskill**, the **Lincoln Society of Dayton**, and even the **Association of Lincoln Presenters**. Lincoln groups also exist is such far-off locales as Taiwan and Japan.

In addition, you can visit memorial sites at virtually every place Lincoln lived. The **Abraham Lincoln Birthplace National Historic Park** in Hodgenville, Kentucky, is run by the National Park Service and includes a neo-classical temple surrounding a recreated "symbolic birth cabin." You can also visit the **Lincoln Boyhood National Memorial** site in Lincoln City, Indiana, and view a replica homestead of where he spent his formative teenage years, as well as the gravesite of his mother, Nancy Hanks. In Illinois, you can visit the village of **New Salem**, a recreation of the frontier village where Lincoln lived the first six years of his time out on his own. From there, go to Springfield where you can get a guided tour through the actual **house in which Lincoln and his family lived**. As with the others, this site is run by the National Park Service. Nearby are **Lincoln's law office**, the **Old State House**, and many other Lincoln-related sites. A few blocks away is the **Abraham Lincoln Presidential Library and Museum**, a sprawling two-building complex providing both an interactive museum of Lincoln's life and, for researchers, one of the best libraries of Lincoln papers outside of Washington. Before leaving Springfield, visit the obelisk of **Lincoln's Tomb** in Oak Ridge Cemetery. Later, if you are into scholarly research, you can visit the **Library of Congress** and **National Archives** collections in Washington, D.C. Many papers are also now digitized and can be searched online. Further reading and resources can be found beginning on page 242.

Monuments to Abraham Lincoln exist nearly everywhere Lincoln set foot during his short fifty-six years of life. Lincoln is one of the four sixty-foot-tall heads carved into Mount Rushmore in the Black Hills of South Dakota (alongside

George Washington, Thomas Jefferson, and Theodore Roosevelt). In addition to the classically styled Lincoln Memorial, there are numerous other statues and commemorations of Lincoln in Washington, D.C. In Springfield, Illinois, and surrounding areas there are hundreds of statues of Lincoln, many of which can be seen at Looking for Lincoln National Heritage Area sites. Lincoln has also been honored internationally with statues in Scotland, England, Mexico, Cuba, and Norway.

No other president has had such a lasting impact on America and indeed the world. Abraham Lincoln saved the Union, emancipated the slaves, and both started and served symbolically as a contributor to civil rights. His faith in the American people has remained an inspiration to young and old, across party lines, for more than 150 years. Perhaps to survive our own struggles in the modern era we should remind ourselves of how Lincoln viewed his situation:

> *Fellow-citizens, we cannot escape history....The fiery trial through*
> *which we pass, will light us down, in honor or dishonor, to the latest*
> *generation. We say we are for the Union. The world will not forget that*
> *we say this. We know how to save the Union....In giving freedom to*
> *the slave, we assure freedom to the free—honorable alike in what we*
> *give, and what we preserve. We shall nobly save, or meanly lose, the last*
> *best, hope of earth. Other means may succeed; this could not fail.*[10]

As Lincoln gave his second inaugural address in March 1865, a twenty-foot-tall bronze Statue of Freedom towered atop the newly completed cast iron dome on the U.S. Capitol. Through four grueling years of war, Lincoln had saved America. Today, his legacy demands that Americans ensure that "government of the people, by the people, for the people, shall not perish from the earth."

OPPOSITE: Portrait of Lincoln by Howard Pyle

THROUGH THE PEEP-HOLE HE HAD BORED IN
R OF THE PRESIDENTIAL BOX, THE MURDER-
D SEE THE BACK OF LINCOLN'S HEAD AS HE
D THE PLAY.

EADLY LITTLE DERRINGER SPAT OUT ITS
E BULLET --- WITH A NOISE LIKE A LOUD HAND

ENTLY, HE OPENED THE DOOR AND STEPPED I
WEAPON COMING UP TO AIM! NOBODY WAS A\
HIS ENTRANCE! BOOTH MOVED ALONG THE W
GET A CLEAR SHOT.

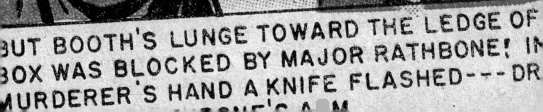

BUT BOOTH'S LUNGE TOWARD THE LEDGE OF
BOX WAS BLOCKED BY MAJOR RATHBONE! IN
MURDERER'S HAND A KNIFE FLASHED---DR

Timeline

1806	June 12, Thomas Lincoln marries Nancy Hanks
1807	February 10, Sarah Lincoln (sister) born
1809	February 12, Abraham Lincoln born in a one-room log cabin on Sinking Spring farm near Hodgenville, Kentucky
1811	Family moves to Knob Creek farm ten miles from Sinking Spring
1812	Brother Thomas born, but lives only three days
1816	Family moves across Ohio River to Little Pigeon Creek in Indiana
1818	October 5, Lincoln's mother dies of "milk sickness"
1819	December 2, Thomas Lincoln marries Sarah Bush Johnston (Lincoln's stepmother) in Kentucky; she moves with her three children to Indiana
1828	January 20, Lincoln's sister, Sarah Lincoln Grigsby, dies in childbirth
1828	Lincoln makes first flatboat trip to New Orleans
1830	Family moves to Illinois, settles on uncleared land on north bank of Sangamon River near Decatur
1831	Second flatboat trip to New Orleans
1831	Family moves again but Lincoln separates and moves to New Salem
1832	Runs for first political office (Illinois General Assembly) at age 23; loses
1832	Serves in Black Hawk War
1833	In January, buys General Store on credit with William F. Berry; it fails by spring. In May he is appointed postmaster. In the fall, becomes Deputy Surveyor
1834	August 4, elected to Illinois General Assembly at age 24 (serves four consecutive terms)
1835	August 25, Ann Rutledge, Lincoln's first love, dies at age 22
1836	September 9, gets license to practice law
1837	March 1, admitted to Illinois bar. Later in year begins riding the Eighth Judicial Circuit, which he will do twice per year every year until he becomes president
1837	April 15, Lincoln moves to Springfield, site of the new state capital. Begins law partnership with John Todd Stuart
1839	Meets Mary Todd and begins courtship
1841	March 1, ends first partnership and begins second law partnership with Stephen T. Logan
1842	November 4, marries Mary Todd
1843	August 3, first son, Robert Todd Lincoln, born
1844	In May, purchases a house in Springfield, Illinois. In December, dissolves partnership with Logan and opens up his own law practice, taking on William H. Herndon as junior partner

1846	March 10, second son, Edward "Eddie" Baker Lincoln born. On August 3, Lincoln is elected as a Whig to the U.S. Congress
1847	Lincoln moves to Washington with Mary and two sons. On December 6, Lincoln takes his seat in the House of Representatives. On December 22, he presents his "Spot Resolutions" challenging President Polk to name the spot that began the Mexican War
1848	Campaigns for General Zachary Taylor as Whig nominee for president
1849	May 22, Lincoln granted U.S. Patent #6469 for a device to buoy vessels over shoals. At end of one term in Congress, Lincoln leaves politics to practice law full time in Springfield
1850	February 4, Eddie Lincoln dies a month before his fourth birthday. On December 21, third son, William "Willie" Wallace Lincoln, is born
1851	January 17, Lincoln's father, Thomas Lincoln, dies
1853	April 4, fourth son, Thomas "Tad" Lincoln is born and named after Lincoln's father
1855	Lincoln re-enters politics after 1854 Kansas–Nebraska Act opens up expansion of slavery into the territories. Runs for U.S. Senate but loses
1856	Campaigns for new Republican Party nominee, John C. Fremont, for president (he loses)
1857	U.S. Supreme Court issues "Dred Scott" decision, effectively allowing slavery to expand into territories (and potentially into all free states). On June 6, Lincoln gives a speech against the decision
1858	June 16, Lincoln receives Republican nomination for U.S. Senate. Gives "House Divided" speech at convention. Engages in series of seven debates with Stephen A. Douglas
1859	Illinois legislature elects Douglas as U.S. senator, 54–46, despite Republicans getting more popular votes
1860	February 27, gives Cooper Union speech in New York City. In March, Lincoln–Douglas debates are published in book form. On May 18, Lincoln receives nomination for president at Republican Convention in Chicago
1860	November 6, Lincoln is elected sixteenth president of the United States. On December 20, South Carolina secedes from Union, followed within two months by Mississippi, Florida, Alabama, Georgia, Louisiana, and Texas
1861	March 4, Lincoln is inaugurated. On April 12, Fort Sumter fired upon in Charleston, North Carolina, harbor. Civil War starts. On April 15, Lincoln calls for 75,000 volunteers for the Union Army. Virginia, Arkansas, North Carolina, and Tennessee secede
1861	July 21, after an initial apparent victory, the Union is soundly defeated in the first battle of Bull Run
1862	February 20, Willie Lincoln dies of typhoid at the age of 11
1862	April 16, Lincoln signs into law the abolishment of slavery in the District of Columbia
1862	September 22, Lincoln issues the preliminary Emancipation Proclamation; on December 31, West Virginia (a split-off of Virginia's western counties) becomes the thirty-fifth state and joins the Union
1863	January 1, Lincoln signs the final Emancipation Proclamation, which frees all the slaves in territories held by the Confederacy

1863	July 1–3, the battle of Gettysburg is fought. On July 4, Ulysses S. Grant captures Vicksburg. On November 19, Lincoln delivers the Gettysburg Address dedicating the battlefield
1864	July 11–12, Fort Stevens on the outskirts of Washington is attacked by Confederate forces led by Lt. General Jubal Early. Lincoln is present at the fort during the attack
1864	September 2, General William T. Sherman captures Atlanta, securing a much-needed victory for the Union. He begins his "March to the Sea"
1864	November 8, Lincoln is reelected to a second term, defeating former General George B. McClellan
1865	March 4, Lincoln is inaugurated for second term
1865	April 9, Confederate General Robert E. Lee surrenders to Union General Ulysses S. Grant at Appomattox Courthouse, Virginia
1865	April 14, Lincoln is assassinated at 10:14 p.m. in Ford's Theatre while watching a performance of *Our American Cousin*
1865	April 15, Lincoln dies at 7:22 a.m. in Petersen's boarding house across the street from Ford's Theatre
1865	April 19–21, Lincoln's body lies in state, then begins the long train ride back to Springfield, Illinois, for burial
1865	April 26, the assassin, John Wilkes Booth, is shot to death in a tobacco barn in Virginia
1865	May 4, Lincoln's body is laid to rest in Oak Ridge Cemetery outside Springfield
1871	July 15, Tad dies at the age of 18
1882	July 16, Mary Lincoln dies of a stroke at the age of 63
1926	July 26, Robert T. Lincoln, the only of Lincoln's sons to survive into adulthood, dies

Further Reading and Resources

With more than 15,000 books written on Abraham Lincoln and more published every year, an exhaustive bibliography is impossible. The following is a selected list of resources to consult for learning more about our sixteenth president.

General
(full-life biographies and primary resources)

Basler, Roy P. 1953. *The Collected Works of Abraham Lincoln*. Rutgers University Press. [Collected Works, CW] [This nine-volume set, plus two addendum volumes, is the ultimate resource for most Abraham Lincoln documents. It is also available in searchable format online at http://quod.lib.umich.edu/l/lincoln/.]

Beveridge, Albert. 1928. *Abraham Lincoln 1809–1858*. Houghton Mifflin.

Burlingame, Michael. 2008. *Abraham Lincoln: A Life*. The Johns Hopkins University Press. [This two-volume set is perhaps the most comprehensive contemporary biography of Lincoln's life. An unedited online version is also available on the Knox College website. All page numbers cited refer to the online version at https://www.knox.edu/about-knox/lincoln-studies-center/burlingame-abraham-lincoln-a-life.]

Brookhiser, Richard. 2014. *Founders' Son: A Life of Abraham Lincoln*. Basic Books.

Carwardine, Richard. 2006. *Lincoln: A Life of Purpose and Power*. Alfred A. Knopf.

Donald, David Herbert. 1995. *Lincoln*. Simon & Schuster.

Herndon, William H. and Weik, Jesse W. as Annotated and Edited by Douglas L. Wilson and Rodney O. Davis. 2006. *Herndon's Lincoln*. University of Illinois Press. [Originally published in 1889, this annotated volume provides the best resource available to modern readers.]

Keneally, Thomas. 2003. *Abraham Lincoln*. Lipper/Viking Books.

Miller, William Lee. 2002. *Lincoln's Virtues: An Ethical Biography*. Alfred A. Knopf.

Nicolay, John G. and Hay, John. 1890. *Abraham Lincoln: A History*. The Century Company. [Original ten-volume biography by Lincoln's private secretaries under Robert Lincoln's authority.]

Oates, Stephen B. 1977. *With Malice Toward None: The Life of Abraham Lincoln*. Harper & Row.

Sandburg, Carl. 1944. *The Prairie Years and the War Years* (six-volume Sangamon Edition). Charles Scribner's Sons.

Thomas, Benjamin. 1952. *Abraham Lincoln*. Alfred A Knopf.

Wilson, Douglas L. and Davis, Rodney O. 2016. *Herndon on Lincoln: Letters*. University of Illinois Press.

Wilson, Douglas L. and Davis, Rodney O. 1998. *Herndon's Informants: Letters, Interviews, and Statements about Abraham Lincoln*. University of Illinois Press. [Wilson and Davis annotate the thousands of letters and interviews conducted by William Herndon after Lincoln's death. The ultimate resource.]

Childhood and Education

Bray, Robert. 2010. *Reading with Lincoln*. Southern Illinois University Press.

Brooks, Noah. 1901. *Abraham Lincoln: His Youth and Early Manhood with a Brief Account of His Later Life*. G.P. Putnam's Sons.

Duncan, Kunigunde and D.F. Nickols. 1944. *Mentor Graham: The Man Who Taught Lincoln*. University of Chicago Press.

Hirsch, David and Van Haften, Dan. 2010. *Abraham Lincoln and the Structure of Reason*. Savas Beatie.

Kirkham, Samuel. 1999. *Kirkham's Grammar: The Book That Shaped Lincoln's Prose*. Octavo Press.

Warren, Louis A. 1959. *Lincoln's Youth: Indiana Years Seven to Twenty-One 1816–1830*. Appleton Century Crofts, Inc.

New Salem

Baber, Adin. 2002. *A. Lincoln with Compass and Chain*. Illinois Professional Land Surveyors Association.

Campanella, Richard. 2010. *Lincoln in New Orleans: The 1828–1831 Flatboat Voyages and Their Place in History*. University of Louisiana at Lafayette Press.

Crump, Thomas. 2009. *Abraham Lincoln's World: How Riverboats, Railroads, and Republicans Transformed America*. Continuum Books.

Illinois Historic Preservation Agency. 2010. *New Salem State Historic Site brochure*.

Rice, Allen Thorndike. 1886. *Reminiscences of Abraham Lincoln*. North American Publishing Company.

Silvestri, Vito N. and Lairo, Alfred P. 2013. *Abraham Lincoln's Intellectual Development 1809–1837*. Wasteland Press.

Spears, Zarel C. and Barton, Robert S. 1947. *Berry and Lincoln Frontier Merchants: The Store That "Winked Out."* Stratford House, Inc.

Politics

Blumenthal, Sidney. 2016. *A Self-Made Man 1809–1849: The Political Life of Abraham Lincoln*. Simon & Schuster.

Crissey, Elwell. 1967. *Lincoln's Lost Speech*. Hawthorn Books, Inc. Donald, David Herbert. 1948. *Lincoln's Herndon*. Alfred A. Knopf.

DeRose, Chris. 2013. *Congressman Lincoln: The Making of America's Greatest President*. Threshold Editions.

Goodwin, Doris Kearns. 2005. *Team of Rivals: The Political Genius of Abraham Lincoln*. Simon & Schuster.

Hanna, William F. 1983. *Abraham Among the Yankees: Abraham Lincoln's 1848 Visit to Massachusetts*. The Old Colony Historical Society.

Harris, William C. 2007. *Lincoln's Rise to the Presidency*. University Press of Kansas.

Kent, David J. 2015. "The Majesty and the Math of Niagara Falls." The Lincolnian. XXXIII: 10–14.

Krenkel, John H. 1958. *Illinois Internal Improvements 1818–1848*. The Torch Press.

Simon, Paul. 1971. *Lincoln's Preparation for Greatness: The Illinois Legislative Years*. University of Illinois Press.

Temple, Wayne C. 1986. *Lincoln's Connections with the Illinois Michigan Canal, His Return From Congress in '48, and His Invention*. Illinois Bell.

Waugh, John C. 1997. *Reelecting Lincoln: The Battle for the 1864 Presidency*. Crown Publishers.

Wilson, Douglas L. 1998. *Honor's Voice: The Transformation of Abraham Lincoln*. Alfred A. Knopf.

Loves and Family Life

Babcock, Bernie. 1919. *The Soul of Ann Rutledge: Abraham Lincoln's Romance*. Grosset & Dunlap.

Baker, Jean H. 1987. *Mary Todd Lincoln: A Biography*. W.W. Norton & Company.

Burlingame, Michael. 1994. *The Inner World of Abraham Lincoln*. University of Illinois Press.

Clinton, Catherine. 2009. *Mrs. Lincoln: A Life*. Harper Collins Publishers.

Donald, David Herbert. 1999. *Lincoln at Home*. Simon & Schuster.

Epstein, Daniel Mark. 2008. *The Lincolns: Portrait of a Marriage*. Ballantine Books.

Fleischner, Jennifer. 2003. *Mrs. Lincoln and Mrs. Keckley: The Remarkable Story of the Friendship Between a First Lady and a Former Slave*. Broadway Books.

Helm, Katherine. 1928. *The True Story of Mary, Wife of Lincoln*. Harper & Brothers Publishers.

Randall, Ruth Painter. 1955. *Lincoln's Sons*. Little, Brown & Company.

Temple, Wayne C. 1995. *Abraham Lincoln: From Skeptic to Prophet*. Mayhaven Publishing.

Walsh, John Evangelist. 2009. *The Shadows Rise: Abraham Lincoln and the Ann Rutledge Legend*. University of Illinois Press.

Weik, Jesse W. 1922. *The Real Lincoln: A Portrait*. Houghton Mifflin Company.

Wilson, Douglas L. 1998. *Honor's Voice: The Transformation of Abraham Lincoln*. Alfred A. Knopf.

Lawyer

Dirck, Brian. 2007. *Lincoln the Lawyer*. University of Illinois Press.

Donald, David Herbert. 2003. *We Are Lincoln Men: Abraham Lincoln and His Friends*. Simon & Schuster.

Fraker, Guy C. 2012. *Lincoln's Ladder to the Presidency: The Eighth Judicial Court*. Southern Illinois University Press.

Hill, Frederick Trevor. 1928. *Lincoln the Lawyer*. The Century Company.

Kent, David J. 2015. *Abraham Lincoln and Nikola Tesla: Connected by Fate*. E-book available at https://www.amazon.com/dp/B014DXOCO4.

McGinty, Brian. 2008. *Lincoln and the Court*. Harvard University Press.

Spiegel, Allen D. 2002. *A. Lincoln: Esquire: A Shrewd, Sophisticated Lawyer in His Time*. Mercer University Press.

Steiner, Mark E. 2006. *An Honest Calling: The Law Practice of Abraham Lincoln*. Northern Illinois University Press.

Whitney, Henry C. 1940. *Life on the Circuit with Lincoln*. The Caxton Printers Ltd.

Woldman, Albert A. 1936. *Lawyer Lincoln*. Carroll & Graf Publishers.

Slavery

Foner, Eric. 2010. *The Fiery Trial: Abraham Lincoln and American Slavery*. W.W. Norton Inc.

Gates, Henry Louis, Jr. 2009. *Lincoln on Race and Slavery*. Princeton University Press.

Guelzo, Allen C. 2004. *Lincoln's Emancipation Proclamation: The End of Slavery in America*. Simon & Schuster.

Guelzo, Allen C. 2008. *Lincoln and Douglas: The Debates That Defined America*. Simon & Schuster.

Holzer, Harold. 2012. *Lincoln: How Abraham Lincoln Ended Slavery in America*. Newmarket Press.

Keckley, Elizabeth. 1989. *Behind the Scenes: Thirty Years a Slave, and Four Years in the White House*. Oxford University Press.

Kendrick, Paul and Stephen Kendrick. 2008. *Douglass and Lincoln: How a Revolutionary Black Leader and a Reluctant Liberator Struggled to End Slavery and Save the Union*. Walker and Company.

Lehrman, Lewis E. 2008. *Lincoln at Peoria: The Turning Point*. Stackpole Books.

Lubet, Steven. 2010. *Fugitive Justice: Runaways, Rescuers, and Slavery on Trial*. The Belknap Press of Harvard University Press.

Maltz, Earl M. 2009. *Slavery and the Supreme Court, 1825–1861*. University Press of Kansas.

Simon, James F. 2006. *Lincoln and Chief Justice Taney: Slavery, Succession, and the President's War Powers*. Simon & Schuster.

Striner, Richard. 2006. *Father Abraham: Lincoln's Relentless Struggle to End Slavery*. Oxford University Press.

President and Civil War

Bates, David Homer. 1995. *Lincoln in the Telegraph Office*. University of Nebraska Press.

Boritt, Gabor. 2006. *The Gettysburg Gospel: The Lincoln Speech That Nobody Knows*. Simon & Schuster.

Brownstein, Elizabeth Smith. 2005. *Lincoln's Other White House: The Untold Story of the Man and His Presidency*. John Wiley & Sons.

Bruce, Robert V. 1956. *Lincoln and the Tools of War*. The Bobbs-Merrill Company.

Carnahan, Burrus M. 2007. *Act of Justice: Lincoln's Emancipation Proclamation and the Law of War*. The University Press of Kentucky.

Conroy, James B. 2014. *Our One Common Country: Abraham Lincoln and the Hampton Roads Peace Conference of 1865*. Lyons Press.

Crofts, Daniel. 2016. *Lincoln and the Politics of Slavery: The Other Thirteenth Amendment and the Struggle to Save the Union*. University of North Carolina Press.

Davis, William C. 1999. *Lincoln's Men: How President Lincoln Became Father to an Army and a Nation*. The Free Press.

Eggleston, Percy Coe. 1943. *Lincoln in New England*. The Tudor Press. Gienapp, William E. 1992. "Abraham Lincoln and the Border States." *Journal of the Abraham Lincoln Association*. 13: 13–46.

Goodwin, Doris Kearns. 2005. *Team of Rivals: The Political Genius of Abraham Lincoln*. Simon & Schuster.

Guelzo, Allen C. 1999. *Abraham Lincoln: Redeemer President*. Wm. B. Eerdmanns Publishing.

Halleck, Henry W. 1862. *Elements of Military Arts and Science*. D. Appleton & Co.

Holzer, Harold. 2008. *Lincoln: President-Elect: Abraham Lincoln and the Great Secession Winter 1860–1861*. Simon & Schuster.

Holzer, Harold. 2014. *Lincoln and the Power of the Press*. Simon & Schuster.

Holzer, Harold. 2004. *Lincoln at Cooper Union*. Simon & Schuster.

Kent, David J. 2014. "A Christmas Gift for Abraham Lincoln." *Smithsonian Civil War Studies* newsletter, December 8, 2014.

McPherson, James M. 2008. *Tried by War: Abraham Lincoln as Commander in Chief*. The Penguin Press.

McPherson, James M. 2002. *Crossroads of Freedom: Antietam*. Oxford University Press.

McPherson, James M. 1988. *Battle Cry of Freedom: The Civil War Era*. Oxford University Press.

Miller, William Lee. 2008. *President Lincoln: The Duty of a Statesman*. Alfred A. Knopf.

Neely, Mark E. Jr. 1991. *The Fate of Liberty: Abraham Lincoln and Civil Liberties*. Oxford University Press.

Oldroyd, Osborn H. 1883. *The Lincoln Memorial: Album-Immortelles*. G.W. Carleton & Co. Press.

Robertson, James I. 1997. *Stonewall Jackson: The Man, The Soldier, The Legend*. Macmillan.

Trudeau, Noah Andre. 1991. *The Last Citadel, June 1864–April 1865*. Savas Beatie.

Trudeau, Noah Andre. 2016. *Lincoln's Greatest Journey: Sixteen Days that Changed a Presidency, March 24–April 8, 1865*. Savas Beatie.

Weber, Jennifer L. 2006. *Copperheads: The Rise and Fall of Lincoln's Opponents in the North*. Oxford University Press.

White, Jonathan W. 2011. *Abraham Lincoln and Treason in the Civil War: The Trials of John Merryman*. Louisiana State University Press.

White, Ronald C. Jr. 2005. *The Eloquent President: A Portrait of Lincoln Through His Words*. Random House.

White, Jonathan W. 2014. *Emancipation, The Union Army, and the Reelection of Abraham Lincoln*. Louisiana State University Press.

Wills, Garry. 1992. *Lincoln at Gettysburg: The Words that Remade America*. Simon & Schuster.

Assassination and Legacy

Alford, Terry. 2015. *Fortune's Fool: The Life of John Wilkes Booth*. Oxford University Press.

Bishop, Jim. 1955. *The Day Lincoln Was Shot*. Harper & Brothers Publishers.

Hodes, Martha. 2015. *Mourning Lincoln*. Yale University Press.

Lewis, Lloyd. 1994. *The Assassination of Lincoln: History and Myth*. MJF Books.

Steers, Edward Jr. 2001. *Blood on the Moon: The Assassination of Abraham Lincoln*. The University Press of Kentucky.

Steers, Edward Jr. 2010. *The Lincoln Assassination Encyclopedia*. Harper Perennial.

Turner, Thomas Reed. 1991. *Beware the People Weeping: Public Opinion and the Assassination of Abraham Lincoln*. Louisiana State University Press.

Swanson, James L. 2006. *Manhunt: The 12-Day Chase for Lincoln's Killer*. William Morrow.

Abraham Lincoln
Organizations

Abraham Lincoln Association: http://www.abrahamlincolnassociation.org/Default.aspx

The Lincoln Forum: http://www.thelincolnforum.org/

Abraham Lincoln Institute: http://www.lincoln-institute.org/index.html

Lincoln Group of the District of Columbia: http://www.lincolngroup.org/

The Lincoln Group of New York: http://lincolngroupny.org/

Lincoln Group of Boston: http://www.lincolngroupboston.org/home.html

The Lincoln Association of Jersey City: http://thelincolnassociationofjerseycity.com/

Lincoln Fellowship of Pennsylvania: https://lincolnfellowship.wildapricot.org/

Lincoln Society in Peekskill (New York): http://www.lincolnsociety.com/index.html

Lincoln Society of Dayton (Ohio): http://www.lincolnsocietyofdayton.org/index.html

The Association of Lincoln Presenters: http://www.lincolnpresenters.net/index.html

Museums/Libraries

Lincoln Heritage Museum: http://www.lincolncollege.edu/museum/explore/

The Lincoln Memorial Shrine: http://www.lincolnshrine.org/

Abraham Lincoln Presidential Library and Museum: http://www.alplm.org/

Ford's Theatre: http://www.fords.org/

Abraham Lincoln's Long Nine Museum: http://www.abrahamlincolnlongninemuseum.com/

Digital Research Collections

Abraham Lincoln Online: http://abrahamlincolnonline.org/

Abraham Lincoln Papers at the Library of Congress: https://memory.loc.gov/ammem/alhtml/malhome.html

Abraham Lincoln Research Site: http://rogerjnorton.com/Lincoln2.html

Collected Works of Abraham Lincoln: http://quod.lib.umich.edu/l/lincoln/

House Divided at Dickinson College: http://housedivided.dickinson.edu/

Knox College: Abraham Lincoln: A Life: https://www.knox.edu/about-knox/lincoln-studies-center/burlingame-abraham-lincoln-a-life

Lincoln Archives Digital Project: http://www.lincolnarchives.us/

Lincoln/Net Online Digital Resources: http://lincoln.lib.niu.edu/

The Law Practice of Abraham Lincoln: http://www.lawpracticeofabrahamlincoln.org/Search.aspx

The Papers of Abraham Lincoln Project: http://www.papersofabrahamlincoln.org/

Lincoln-Related Historic Sites

Birthplace National Historic Park (Kentucky): https://www.nps.gov/abli/index.htm

Lincoln Boyhood National Memorial (Indiana): https://www.nps.gov/libo/index.htm

Lincoln's New Salem State Historic Site: http://www.lincolnsnewsalem.com/

Lincoln Home National Historic Site (Springfield): https://www.nps.gov/liho/index.htm

Lincoln Tomb State Historic Site: http://www.lincolntomb.org/

Looking for Lincoln National Heritage Area: http://www.lookingforlincoln.com/

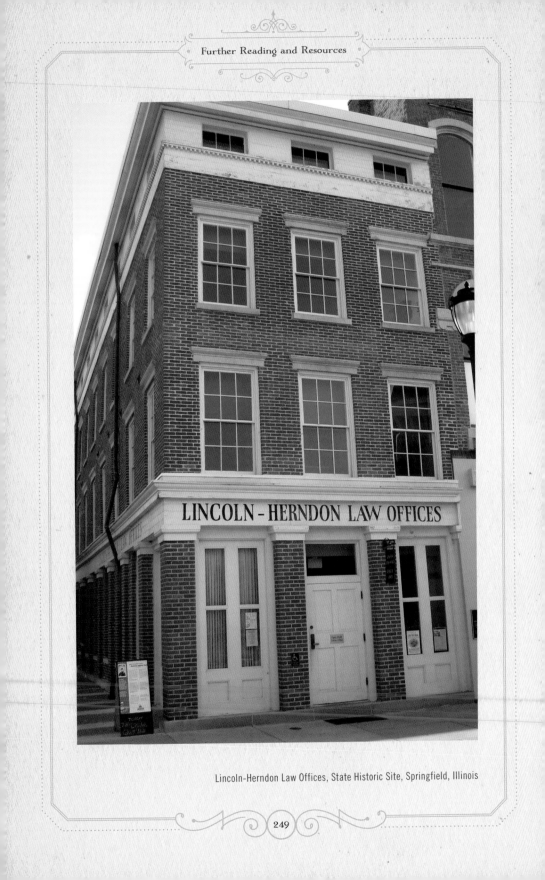

Lincoln-Herndon Law Offices, State Historic Site, Springfield, Illinois

Endnotes

Preface

1 Basler. 1953. *Collected Works of Abraham Lincoln* (hereafter *CW*). Volume 4, pp. 263–71 (hereafter 4: 263–271).

Chapter 1: Kentucky Born, Indiana Raised

1 Donald. 1995. *Lincoln*.

2 *CW.* 4:60–8.

3 See Burlingame. 2008. *Abraham Lincoln: A Life* (hereafter *A Life*). p. 31

4 Burlingame. *A Life*. p. 6.

5 Wilson and Davis. 2016. *Herndon on Lincoln: Letters* (hereafter *Herndon's Letters*).

6 *A Life*. p. 44.

7 Herndon and Weik. 2006. *Herndon's Lincoln* (hereafter *Herndon's Lincoln*). p. 22.

8 Donald. *Lincoln*. pp. 22–3; Sandburg, Carl. 1944. *The Prairie Years and the War Years*. pp. 15–20.

9 *CW.* 4:60–8.

10 Burlingame. *A Life*. p. 51.

11 *CW.* 4:62.

12 Warren. 1959. *Lincoln's Youth Indiana Years, Seven to Twenty-One 1816–1830*. p. 12.

13 *CW.* 4:60–8.

14 Donald, *Lincoln*. pp. 24–5; Burlingame, *A Life*.

15 Burlingame, *A Life*. pp. 87–9.

16 Herndon, *Herndon's Lincoln*; http://www.bartleby.com/73/1225.html.

17 Burlingame, *A Life*. pp. 94–9.

18 See https://www.nps.gov/libo/learn/historyculture/thomaslincoln.htm

19 Burlingame, *A Life*. pp. 98–9.

20 *CW.* 4:60–8.

21 Burlingame, *A Life*. p. 39.

22 Warren. *Lincoln's Youth*. p. 11.

23 *CW.* 3:511.

24 *CW.* 4:60–8.

25 Bray. 2010. *Reading with Lincoln*. p. 4.

26 Warren. *Lincoln's Youth*. pp. 161–2.

27 *CW.* 6:393.

28 Bray, *Reading with Lincoln*. p. 194.

29 *CW.* 4:62.

30 Burlingame, *A Life*. pp. 150–2; Wilson and Davis. 1998. *Herndon's Informants: Letters Interviews, and Statements About Abraham Lincoln* (hereafter *Herndon's Informants*). p. 131.

Chapter 2: Coming of Age in Illinois

1 Burlingame, *A Life*. pp. 154–8.

2 *Herndon's Informants*. p. 104.

3 *CW.* 4:63; Warren, *Lincoln's Youth*; Burlingame, *A Life*. pp. 169–178.

4 For flatboat trips, see
Campanella. 2010. *Lincoln in
New Orleans.* pp. 143–160;
CW. 4:63–4; Crump. 2009.
*Abraham Lincoln's World:
How Riverboats, Railroads, and
Republicans Transformed America.*
pp. 23–34.

5 For time in New Salem, see
Illinois Historic Preservation
Agency brochure; Burlingame,
A Life. pp. 195–205; personal
communication with Jim
Patton, retired lead interpreter,
September 30, 2016.

6 Burlingame, *A Life.* pp. 205–206;
Herndon's Informants. p. 18.

7 Burlingame, *A Life.* p. 206;
Herndon's Informants. p. 9.

8 *CW.* 3:512.

9 Rice. 1886. *Reminiscences of
Abraham Lincoln.* pp. 218–9.

10 For discussion of the store,
see Spears and Barton. *Berry
and Lincoln Frontier Merchants:
The Store That "Winked Out."*
1947; Illinois Historic
Preservation Agency brochure;
Burlingame, *A Life.* pp. 258–262.

11 *CW.* 4:65.

12 Burlingame, *A Life.* pp. 264–5.

13 *CW.* 4:65.

14 Baber. 2002. *A. Lincoln with
Compass and Chain.* pp. 2–4.

Chapter 3: Beginning a Life in Politics

1 Oates. 1977. *With Malice Toward
None: The Life of Abraham Lincoln*
(hereafter *Malice*). pp. 18–20;

Burlingame, *A Life.* pp. 229–230;
quote from *Herndon's Informants.*
pp. 384–5.

2 *CW.* 1:5–9.

3 *CW.* 3:29.

4 *CW.* 1:5–9.

5 *CW.* 4:64.

6 Burlingame, *A Life.* p. 285–6.

7 Quote in Rice, *Reminiscences.*
p. 466. Also see Burlingame,
A Life. p. 296; Donald, *Lincoln.*
pp. 52–3.

8 *Herndon's Informants.* p. 254.

9 Simon. 1971. *Lincoln's Preparation
for Greatness* (hereafter *Preparation*).
p, 21; Donald, *Lincoln.* p. 75;
CW. 1:29; Burlingame, *A Life.*
p. 320.

10 Oates, *Malice.* p. 34; Burlingame,
A Life. p. 379; Simon, *Preparation.*
pp. 46–7.

11 Krenkel. 1958. *Illinois Internal
Improvements.* pp. 26–46; Temple.
1986. *Lincoln's Connections with the
Illinois Michigan Canal* (hereafter
Connections). pp. 1–8.

12 *Herndon's Informants.* p. 476;
Temple, *Connections.* p. 6.

13 Burlingame, *A Life.* p. 342.

14 Burlingame, *A Life,* pp. 377–8.

15 Simon, *Preparation.* pp. 20–23;
Burlingame, *A Life.* pp. 315–7.

16 *Herndon's Informants.* p. 465.

17 Oates, *Malice.* pp. 34–5.

18 *CW.* 7:281.

19 *CW.* 1:75.

20 DeRose. 2013. *Congressman Lincoln*; Burlingame, *A Life*. Chapter 8.

21 DeRose, *Congressman Lincoln*. p. 123; Burlingame, *A Life*. p. 755.

22 Burlingame, *A Life*. pp. 777–792; DeRose, *Congressman Lincoln*, p. 259.

23 Hanna. 1983. *Abraham Among the Yankees*; Kent. 2015. "Abraham Lincoln: The Majesty and the Math of Niagara Falls," *The Lincolnian*, Sept./Oct. 2015, pp. 10–14.

Chapter 4: Lincoln's Love and Family

1 Quotes in this paragraph from Wilson. 1998. *Honor's Voice*. p. 109; Burlingame, *A Life*. p. 327; *Herndon's Informants*. p. 541; Burlingame. 1994. *The Inner World of Abraham Lincoln* (hereafter *Inner World*). p. 123.

2 Wilson, *Honor's Voice*. pp. 109–11.

3 Burlingame, *A Life*. p. 328.

4 *Herndon's Informants*. p. 606; Burlingame. pp. 329–330.

5 Walsh. 2009. *The Shadows Rise*; Wilson, *Honor's Voice*. pp. 114–8; Burlingame, *A Life*. pp. 330–5.

6 *Herndon's Informants*. p. 440.

7 *Herndon's Informants*. p. 383, 556–7; Wilson, *Honor's Voice*. p. 116; Burlingame, *A Life*. p. 337.

8 *CW.* 1:117.

9 Walsh, *The Shadows Rise*. pp. 111–22; Burlingame, *A Life*. pp. 516–8; *Herndon's Informants* p. 256.

10 Two quote blocks: *CW.* 1:118–9.

11 Two quote blocks *Herndon's Informants*. pp. 589–90; Burlingame, *A Life*. pp. 415–6.

12 Clinton. 2009. *Mrs. Mary Lincoln: A Life* (hereafter *Mrs. Mary Lincoln*). pp. 11–17.

13 Baker. 1987. *Mary Todd Lincoln*. pp. 40–41; Helm. 1928. *The True Story of Mary, Wife of Lincoln* (hereafter *True Story*). pp. 1–2; Donald, *Lincoln*. p. 85.

14 Helm, *True Story*. pp. 62–3; *Herndon's Informants*. p. 446; Burlingame, *A Life*. pp. 520–3.

15 Wilson, *Honor's Voice*. pp. 219–24; Burlingame, *A Life*. pp. 542–3; *Herndon's Informants*. p. 444.

16 Weik. 1922. *The Real Lincoln*. pp. 67–8; Burlingame, *Inner World*. p. 135.

17 *CW.* 1:305; *Herndon's Informants*. p. 444; Burlingame, *A Life*. pp. 588–9; Temple. 1995. *Abraham Lincoln From Skeptic to Prophet* (hereafter *Skeptic to Prophet*). pp. 27–8.

18 Donald. 1999. *Lincoln at Home*. pp. 59–60.

Chapter 5: Life as a Lawyer

1 *CW.* 4:65; Warren. *Lincoln's Youth*. pp. 146–7; Dirck. 2007. *Lincoln the Lawyer*. pp. 15–6; Burlingame, *A Life*. pp. 294–5.

2 *CW.* 4:121.

3 Dirck, *Lincoln the Lawyer*. pp. 16–20; *CW*. 4:65–6; *CW*. 4:121; Burlingame, *A Life*. p. 300; Bray, *Reading with Lincoln*. pp. 223–9.

4 Dirck, *Lincoln the Lawyer*. p. 24.

5 Dirck, *Lincoln the Lawyer*. pp. 60–61.

6 Donald. *Lincoln*. p. 98.

7 Donald, *Lincoln*. pp. 97–100; Burlingame, *A Life*. p. 300.

8 *Herndon's Lincoln*; Dirck, *Lincoln the Lawyer*. p. 60; Donald, *Lincoln*. p. 99.

9 Donald. 2003. *We Are Lincoln Men* (hereafter *Lincoln Men*). pp. 67–8; Illinois Historic Preservation Agency brochure.

10 Donald. 1948. *Lincoln's Herndon*. pp. 18–21; Donald, *Lincoln Men*. pp. 68–9; Donald, *Lincoln*. pp. 100–2.

11 Whitney. 1940. *Life on the Circuit*.

12 Fraker. 2012. *Lincoln's Ladder to the Presidency* (hereafter *Lincoln's Ladder*); Burlingame, *A Life*. p. 418.

13 Fraker, *Lincoln's Ladder*. p. 67; Donald, *Lincoln*. pp. 104–6.

14 Burlingame, *A Life*. p. 470; Fraker, *Lincoln's Ladder*. p. 1.

15 *CW*. 2:82.

16 Steiner. 2006. *An Honest Calling*. pp. 4, 15, 160.

17 Spiegel. 2002. *A. Lincoln, Esquire* (hereafter *Esquire*). p. ix.

18 This case, Spiegel, *Esquire*. pp. 155–60.

19 Dirck, *Lincoln the Lawyer*. p. 88.

20 *CW*. 2:32–5.

21 Kent. 2015. *Abraham Lincoln and Nikola Tesla: Connected by Fate* (hereafter *Connected*).

22 This case, Spiegel, *Esquire*. pp. 96–8.

23 Dirck, *Lincoln the Lawyer*. pp. 147–8; Fraker, *Lincoln's Ladder*. p. 52.

24 Steiner, *An Honest Calling*. pp. 102–23; Fraker, *Lincoln's Ladder*. pp. 50–1; Dirck, *Lincoln the Lawyer*. pp. 148–9.

Chapter 6: A House Divided—Slavery on the Rise

1 *CW*. 4:67.

2 *CW*. 1:75.

3 *CW*. 2:498.

4 Foner. 2010. *The Fiery Trial: Abraham Lincoln and American Slavery*; Holzer. 2012. *Lincoln: How Abraham Lincoln Ended Slavery*; Lubet. 2010. *Fugitive Justice*; Maltz. 2009. *Slavery and the Supreme Court*; Simon. 2006. *Lincoln and Chief Justice Taney*; Striner. 2006. *Father Abraham*.

5 Burlingame, *A Life*. p. 1093.

6 Lehrman. 2008. *Lincoln at Peoria*.

7 *CW*. 2:255.

8 *CW*. 2:266.

9 *CW*. 2:461.

10 Burlingame, *A Life*. p. 1297.

11 Guelzo. 2008. *Lincoln and Douglas: The Debates That Defined America.*

12 Burlingame, *A Life*. pp. 1351–5.

13 *CW*. 3:29.

14 *CW*. 3:145–6.

15 *CW*. 3:43.

Chapter 7: Running for President

1 Oldroyd. 1883. *The Lincoln Memorial: Album–Immortelles* (hereafter *Immortelles*). pp. 473–6; Burlingame, *A Life*. pp. 1523–6.

2 Burlingame, *A Life*. p. 1568.

3 Burlingame, *A Life*. p. 1553.

4 *CW*. 3:512; Blumenthal. 2016. *A Self-Made Man 1809–1849* (hereafter *Self-Made Man*).

5 Holzer. 2004. *Lincoln at Cooper Union* (hereafter *Cooper Union*); Burlingame, *A Life*. pp. 1588–1606.

6 For Cooper Union speech, see Holzer, *Cooper Union*. pp. 111, 120–131.

7 Holzer, *Cooper Union*. pp. 116, 131–9; *CW* 3:522–50.

8 *CW*. 3:550.

9 Eggleston. 1943. *Lincoln in New England*. pp. 7–9; Burlingame, *A Life*, pp. 1610–1.

10 Holzer. 2014. *Lincoln and the Power of the Press* (hereafter *Power of the Press*); Burlingame, *A Life*. pp. 1584–5.

11 *Herndon's Informants*. p. 463; Burlingame, *A Life*. pp. 1633–6.

12 Burlingame, *A Life*. pp. 1586–7.

13 Burlingame, *A Life*. pp. 1644–8.

14 *CW*. 4:34.

15 Burlingame, *A Life*. pp. 1718–36.

16 *CW*. 4:190.

17 *CW*. 4:240.

Chapter 8: Preserving the Union

1 Donald, *Lincoln*. p. 267; Burlingame, *A Life*. pp. 1843–5, 1872; Crofts. 2016. *Lincoln and the Politics of Slavery*; Crofts, personal communication; Holzer. 2008. *Lincoln: President-Elect.*

2 *CW*. 4:271.

3 Goodwin. 2005. *Team of Rivals.*

4 Neely. 1991. *The Fate of Liberty*. pp. 3–31; White. 2011. *Abraham Lincoln and Treason in the Civil War.*

5 Donald, *Lincoln*. pp. 432–6.

6 Robertson. 1997. *Stonewall Jackson: The Man, the Soldier, the Legend*. p. 739

7 Donald, *Lincoln*. pp. 318–9; McPherson. 1988. *Battle Cry of Freedom* (hereafter *Battle Cry*). p. 364.

8 Donald, *Lincoln*. pp. 349–52.

9 McPherson. 2002. *Crossroads of Freedom: Antietam* (hereafter *Crossroads*). p. 100.

10 *CW*. 5:473.

11 McPherson, *Crossroads*. p. 3.

12 Donald, *Lincoln*. pp. 314–7; Oates, *Malice*. p. 260; Carwardine. 2006. *Lincoln: A Life of Purpose and Power* (hereafter *Life of Purpose*). p. 181; Guelzo. 1999. *Abraham Lincoln: Redeemer President*. pp. 290–1.

13 Keckley. 1989. *Behind the Scenes: Thirty Years a Slave, and Four Years in the White House* (hereafter *Behind the Scenes*).

14 Gienapp. 1992. "Abraham Lincoln and the Border States." *JALA*. pp. 13–46.

15 Guelzo. 2004. *Lincoln's Emancipation Proclamation*.

16 *CW*. 5:388.

Chapter 9: From Gettysburg to Re-election

1 *CW*. 6:78–9.

2 McPherson. *Battle Cry*; McPherson. *Tried by War*.

3 Borritt. 2006. *The Gettysburg Gospel*.

4 *CW*. 6:328.

5 Donald, *Lincoln*. pp. 450–60; Wills. 1992. *Lincoln at Gettysburg*.

6 *CW*. 7:17–23.

7 James Cornelius, Curator, Abraham Lincoln Presidential Library and Museum, Springfield, Illinois. Personal communication, September 2016.

8 *CW*. 7:499.

9 Donald, *Lincoln*. p. 490–510.

10 Trudeau. 1991. *The Last Citadel*.

11 Donald, *Lincoln*. pp. 516–8.

12 *CW*. 7:419; Also, https://abrahamlincolnandthecivilwar.wordpress.com/2014/06/30/resignation-of-treasury-secretary-salmon-p-chase-is-accepted-washington-shocked/.

13 *CW*. 7:514.

14 White. 2014. *Emancipation, The Union Army, and Reelection*.

15 *CW*. 8:181-2.

16 Kent. 2014. "A Christmas Gift for Abraham Lincoln." *Smithsonian Civil War Studies*.

Chapter 10: Of Martyrdom and Legacy

1 Check out the 2012 movie, *Lincoln*, by Steven Spielberg for a dramatic depiction.

2 Conroy. 2014. *Our Common Country*.

3 McPherson, *Battle Cry*; Trudeau. 2016. *Lincoln's Greatest Journey*.

4 *CW*. 8:332–3.

5 Bishop. 1955. *The Day Lincoln Was Shot*; Swanson. 2006. *Manhunt*; Steers. 2001. *Blood on the Moon*; Steers. 2010. *The Lincoln Assassination Encyclopedia*.

6 Turner. 1991. *Beware the People Weeping*.

7 *CW*. 2:220–1.

8 *CW*. 6:28–30.

9 Kent, *Connected by Fate*.

10 *CW*. 5:537.

ACKNOWLEDGMENTS

I am indebted to a long line of scholars who have spent countless hours transcribing old letters and government documents, just as I am indebted to the modern-day technology wizards who have digitized many of those documents. Any list of acknowledgments for Lincoln studies must begin with the incomparable work of Michael Burlingame, Harold Holzer, Douglas Wilson, and others who have annotated dozens of historic volumes and thousands of primary materials. The service they have provided to all Lincoln researchers is immeasurable.

I have been honored to meet hundreds of Abraham Lincoln scholars and for several years have worked with the amazing people at the Lincoln Group of the District of Columbia (LGDC). Special thanks go out to John Elliff, Rod Ross, Ray Rongley, Buzz Carnahan, Elizabeth Smith Brownstein, Susan Dennis, Craig Howell, Wendy Swanson, and John O'Brien for their insights and encouragement. Very special thanks to members of the LGDC book discussion group, whose monthly discussions over several years have provided endless insights and alternative viewpoints (John Elliff, John O'Brien, Rod Ross, Jon Blackman, John Swallow, Debbie Jackson, Diane Putney, Janet Saros, Susan Hadler, Ted Beal, Dick Meyer, Ed Epstein, and especially Richard Margolies for his adept leadership of the group).

Thank you to the people who made *Tesla: The Wizard of Electricity* and *Edison: The Inventor of the Modern World* such successes that they spawned this opportunity for me to write a book about the man I have spent an entire life admiring. My personal collection of about 1,200 Lincoln books seems small in contrast to the more than 15,000 books written about the man. There never seems to be an end to the knowledge.

I want to thank my agent, Marilyn Allen of Allen O'Shea Literary Agency, and my editor, Chris Barsanti at Fall River Press, Sterling Publishing, for allowing me this opportunity.

Finally, thanks to my friends, family, fellow scientists, fellow Lincoln historians, and fellow writers who have inspired and encouraged both my professional scientific and independent historian careers. Extra special thanks go to Ru Sun for her constant encouragement, constructive criticism, and exceptional attention to detail. This book and I are much better because of her efforts.

As always, I have tried to be accurate in my writing and citations of outside resources. As Lincoln once said:

> However, upon the subjects of which I have treated, I have spoken as I thought. I may be wrong in regard to any or all of them; but holding it a sound maxim, that it is better to be only sometimes right, than at all times wrong, so soon as I discover my opinions to be erroneous, I shall be ready to renounce them.

About the Author

A lifelong independent Lincoln researcher, David J. Kent is currently Vice President of Programs for the Abraham Lincoln Group of Washington, D.C., and an active member of the Abraham Lincoln Association, Abraham Lincoln Institute, and Lincoln Forum. His activities with the Lincoln Group include monthly meetings with Lincoln scholars, active participation in the Lincoln book discussion group, contributions to the newsletter (including a quarterly book-review column), and development of the group's social communications network and blog. His Lincoln writing includes articles for the Smithsonian Civil War Studies website and *The Lincolnian* newsletter. He owns more than 1,200 books about Abraham Lincoln, reads twenty to thirty Lincoln books a year, and conducts extensive research on Abraham Lincoln and his life.

David J. Kent is also an award-winning scientist and author of *Tesla: The Wizard of Electricity* (2013) and *Edison: The Inventor of the Modern World* (2016), both published by Fall River Press. His website can be found at www.davidjkent-writer.com.

Image Credits

MERCURY

EXTRA:

Passed unanimously at 1.15 o'clock, P. M. December 20th, 1860.

AN ORDINANCE

To dissolve the Union between the State of South Carolina and other States united with her under the compact entitled "The Constitution of the United States of America."

We, the People of the State of South Carolina, in Convention assembled, do declare and ordain, and it is hereby declared and ordained,

That the Ordinance adopted by us in Convention, on the twenty-third day of May, in the year of our Lord one thousand seven hundred and eighty-eight, whereby the Constitution of the United States of America was ratified, and also, all Acts and parts of Acts of the General Assembly of this State, ratifying amendments of the said Constitution, are hereby repealed; and that the union now subsisting between South Carolina and other States, under the name of "The United States of America," is hereby dissolved.

THE

UNION

IS

DISSOLVED!